ARTHUR LOWE
A LIFE

Stephen Lowe

ARTHUR LOWE
a life

NICK HERN BOOKS
London

A Nick Hern Book

Arthur Lowe – a Life first published in Great Britain
in 1996 by Nick Hern Books Limited, 14 Larden Road,
London W3 7ST

Copyright © 1996 by Stephen Lowe

Stephen Lowe has asserted his right to be identified
as the author of this work

A CIP catalogue record for this book is available from
the British Library

ISBN 1 85459 279 3

Typeset by Country Setting, Woodchurch, Kent TN26 3TB
Printed and bound in Great Britain by Biddles Ltd,
Guildford and King's Lynn

To Nina Joan Lowe
with love from daddy

Contents

Illustrations

Arthur Lowe at home, 1916 (Tony Oliver Collection)
At Hayfield, c. 1935 (Tony Oliver Collection)
With Daisy, the pony that never saw action
    (Tony Keen Collection)

The desert life (Tony Keen Collection)
A very sharp mind (Tony Oliver Collection)
The Mercury Theatre, Alexandria (Tony Oliver Collection)

The ideal character actor, short and bald
    (Tony Keen Collection)

Joan Cooper (Tony Keen Collection)
Stephen, *A Night To Remember* (Rank)
The roof garden, 33-35 Pavilion Road
    (Keystone/Chris Ware)

Dr Munda, *O Lucky Man!*
    (Copyright © 1973, Warner Bros. Inc.)
Hudson, *Inadmissible Evidence* (Zoë Dominic)

Leonard Swindley, *Coronation Street* (Granada TV)

Captain Mainwaring, relaxing with the irascible crowd

Dogberry, *Much Ado About Nothing*

Acknowledgments

I'd like to thank: Barry State, he knows why; Tony Oliver of TLO Film Services for rescuing the archive from the cellars of a well-known auction house; Tony and Lesley Keen for looking after most of that archive now; Bill Bateman and the DLO Veterans; Ron Heron of Hayfield Cricket Club; and all the people in the business and other friends who wrote or phoned with their memories of Arthur. Thank you all.

S.L.

She loved me for the dangers I had pass'd,
And I loved her that she did pity them.
William Shakespeare, Othello

Hate is like a clown with a knife,
he must draw blood to get the joke.
Edward Bond, Bingo

Prologue

THE morning my father died I was in my bunk aboard the 'Amazon'. Through the open porthole came the scent of the river. It was spring, and everywhere was the sound of birds and ducks, the new cycle on the up-stroke. I lay, contemplating the prospects for the day. I had no premonition. A transistor radio was on in the galley, and I heard the deckhouse clock strike so I knew the time, but there was no hurry, my parents were away on tour. We had boatsy friends staying, and our day would be passed gently painting or varnishing, fixing this or that, having a pint. Big, shambling Shaun came in with mugs of tea and sat on the bunk and still I didn't know.

'Bag, I've got some very bad news. Your Dad has died, they've just announced it on the radio.'

Whatever goes through anybody's mind when they receive news like this – from a policeman at the door, over the phone, gently from an old friend as I had done – they may have a moment of stunning perception, of perfect clarity. In that instant I knew that my father didn't belong to me and hadn't done for years; he had moved into the public domain.

I didn't feel angry at the indiscretion of the BBC. I didn't feel sad, I felt matter-of-fact, normal. No cliché without truth: life went on.

I had another, bigger shock to come. My elder brother was abroad, so I had expected to have to go at once to Birmingham or London, probably by plane. I looked out my rarely worn suit, wondered if I had a black tie. We had many good friends along the river, and the morning was spent receiving sincere condolences from people who came out in boats and felt embarrassed by our loss. I needed to get to a phone, but each of the waterborne mourners deserved our attention. We lowered the ensign to half mast.

When eventually I phoned my mother I was surprised, hurt, outraged, to find that she was utterly in control, needed me not at all. She wanted and would accept no sympathy but informed me that everything was in hand: she had advised the accountant, solicitor and the bank. Bill Bateman would be taking care of the funeral arrangements and she would be continuing with the tour. There was nothing for me to do at present.

'No, there's no point in coming up to Birmingham. Vyvian is looking after me and everyone in the company is being just marvellous.'

Grief controlled with an inner strength frozen into ice that would never shatter into tears. A grief so solely hers she wouldn't let anybody touch it. Not even me. Her strength had shut me out, and, selfishly, I retired hurt. Redundant.

We walked into Cowes, two couples in jeans and jumpers and boat shoes with the toe gone through, bought a paper and went into a pub. I supposed I would now be rich and that I would be able to be more my own man. I wondered about how things would be carved up. Everyone was very kind, they said the country had lost a fine actor, what pleasure he'd given,

how he'd be missed. Various obituaries appeared, some
of which I read:

> Arthur Lowe, the actor best known for his
> portrayal of the pompous Home Guard leader,
> Captain Mainwaring in the television comedy
> series, *Dad's Army*, died yesterday at the age of
> 66. He suffered a stroke in his dressing room at
> the Alexandra Theatre, Birmingham, where he
> was appearing in the play, *Home At Seven*, and
> died later in hospital.
>
> Though his nine years in *Dad's Army* made
> him a national figure, Arthur Lowe had a long
> and distinguished career as a character actor on
> the stage and in films as well as on television.
> His work ranged from Shakespeare to American
> musicals and farce.
>
> He was born in Hayfield, Derbyshire, on 22
> September, 1915, the only son of a railway
> worker, left school at 16 to work in an
> aeroplane factory, and started acting, as an
> amateur, while serving in the army during the
> war. He made his first professional appearance
> with a repertory company in Manchester in
> 1945. A short, rotund man, he wryly remarked
> that premature baldness decided from the age
> of 30 that he should be a character actor rather
> than a romantic lead . . .

I went to the funeral. There were only a handful of us at
the crematorium. My mother was in Ireland with the show.
I watched a coffin – which I could not believe contained
my father – go along a conveyor belt and through

electric curtains which parted automatically and then closed again to piped music. I would rather have burnt his corpse on the riverbank as I'd seen pathetic groups do on the Hooghly, it would have served my grief better. After the funeral I went back aboard the 'Amazon' and hauled the ensign hard up to the truck, and it remained there until it was tattered out to nothing by the salt wind.

Time went by and twelve years after 15 April 1982 I found myself taking off in a plane, soaring upwards in a frozen dawn sky, banking to starboard, turning south toward London. It was incongruous, the pseudo-civility within the plane and the raw elements just the other side of the glass, the Highlands spread out beneath us like old green velvet curtains, the indigo blue of deep space above. I never knew him, he was always out at work, or on the phone, and then I went to boarding school and away to sea. Only now he had gone did I realise that he had been extraordinary and that I had missed my chance. So many people I met wanted to reach out and touch him.

Now I was engaged in a pointless exercise, an empty gesture dreamed up by pop charity, I was lending my support in a drawn-along-on-the-tide sort of way – because I hadn't the heart to spoil their fun. Showbiz is showbiz after all, and placing a blue plaque on your house, or putting a perspex trophy in your hand, you've got to be seen to be honoured. I don't suppose John le Mesurier's heart is staked out in Baron's Court any more than Arthur's was at Little Venice. The shrines are marked now, so the faithful can be sure, yes this is where they lived.

The turn-out wasn't bad, Spike Milligan missed the ceremony for Dad at Maida Avenue, but he just made it for John. Quite a few of the team were there, and the writers. We got in all the papers, Durrant's clipped their way to a fortune. I believe we raised some money for charity, but I can't remember how much, or for whom.

People – strangers – asked me,

'Was he like Captain Mainwaring at home?'

'Did he ever call you stupid boy?'

It was they who wanted this book, not me. Certainly it wasn't Arthur. But I'm glad they asked me because now I've made a journey I had been putting off, and if I cannot say that I have enjoyed it, I have at least gained from it. He would have said,

'How dare you?'

1

'Big Arthur, little Arthur'
1989

THE light came late. I woke with the first crack of it as it crept around the curtains pulled across the windscreen. I could see by the luminous hands of my Ingersoll wristwatch – the one which had reliably measured the ticking away of my life since I was a boy, as relentless as a taximeter in crawling traffic – that it was ten minutes to eight. This did not bode well.

I lay there warm and edgy. Unusually, totally tea coursed through my system because this was England and po-faced jam-sandwich-men didn't see value in a half bottle of wine with a lorry driver's lunch. I picked up my book and was just turning to the page when some ignorant sod banged loudly on the side of my cab. It isn't easy to get out of the little bunks they somehow cram in behind the seats but you get a kind of way of doing it that plonks you straight behind the wheel, ready to go. Only I'd taken off my trousers which was clearly a mistake.

He was a congenial fellow with the dead-pan humour of the dyed-in-the-wool Mancunian and the high, nasal delivery. Something like Don Estelle in overalls.

'One-day wildcat strike. Be back here this time tomorrow.' And without wasting any more breath on tittle-tattle he sugared off. I sat for a while wondering whether I'd have another go at my Harry Houdini impression and I thought not. It must be true that he could dislocate his shoulders at will, even wrapped in chains and locked in a casket under water he seemed to be able to wriggle free.

I opened the door and kicked my shoes down onto the hard ground. I climbed down, my trousers in my teeth. I pulled them on over white hairy legs, hopping from foot to foot, shuffled into my shoes with the backs flat under my heels and walked to the back of the trailer to relieve myself. I was parked up on this bit of cinder yard, just a portacabin and a high fence around stacked drums of toxic chemicals, the raw stuff of industry. That's what I could do, wriggle free – for a day – from python Duty's grip.

I pulled up my zip and started taking the lenses and bulbs off the trailer. I knew already how I'd spend my day. The handle was cold in my hands as I wound down the legs till they just kissed the cinders then back up half-a-turn, jumped up and let off the air lines – sphht, pulled the pin – clank, started up and within five minutes – no card in – I was driving off down the road like a kid skipping school and leaving a plume of white smoke from the stack, lit by the low sun against a leaden sky. I could see this view reflected in my door mirror and a crystal of light glanced off the chrome and struck my eye.

I followed signs for the docks and along an empty cobbled street that led promisingly downwards. Everywhere was shut up or abandoned, even the rats had left.

Then I turned a corner and before me lay the broad stainless band of the Ship Canal. Twenty years since I'd stood like a spare prick – in a uniform so new the brass buttons were not yet turned green – on the foc'sle of a ship sailing for India. Oh, that I could be on that ship now, battered cap and verdigris on three stripes, Urdu flowing off my tongue as freely as the English word. But that ship is no more, nor is that man. Nor was that ever to be.

I drive a little more and I come to a roadhouse. I get tea and toast from a fat woman who asks,

'Is that all, luv?'

After breakfast I set off, I'm going to go home – to Hayfield.

From up here, ten feet above the road, you can see over the hedgerows and the drystone walls. You can count the sheep up a hillside, can see the road way up ahead, and it lets you relax. I'm getting into the Dark Peak now and it's a day ideally suited to the terrain, and to my mood. The clouds are black and laden and low over the tops. Heavy drops of rain have come before the wind.

Kinder Scout is menacing at me and as I drift a bit on a long right hander I realise I'm getting near. Hayfield – it's sprawled since Arthur was born here, but it's much the same old place. I see the black satanic mill down by the river, where dippers jump between the stones at the weir. Getting ready for the junction I can see the church spire and the northern rooftops and chimneys. The main street will be too tight for the unit so I park up in a corner of the bus station. On the edge of memory lane.

As I climb down, pulling on a leather jacket against the rain that is now coming down steadily, I look around. I'm confused because this part of the village has all changed. I struggle to remember it as it was. There are National Park signs and a Visitor Centre, the quango stormtroopers have been. The river flows under the new dual carriageway and I stand and shelter from the rain which is now coming down in stair rods. In spray paint Kirsty loves Paul, but Gary is a queer. Well, if I meet them, at least I'll know the score. A woman walks her dog along the bank and I hear again my mother tongue, the thick dialect of Derbyshire.

'Ee, it's a fine day,' she says.

'It's raining,' I reply.

'Aye, but I've got an oombreller.'

It seems to be easing so I walk along to where the railway station used to be. Before Lord Beeching this was the way in and out of the village; most people, you could say, had not got private cars. The milk train, having returned from the city, would stand at Hayfield through the forenoon and because my Grandad had worked for the Late Never Early Railway Company – all his days, save for when he was in the trenches – I would be allowed up onto the footplate of the hissing loco. The fire was very hot on my fresh face and bare knees and the men made jokes which I didn't understand. When the driver and the fireman called him 'Mr Lowe' I registered the respect he commanded. My father's father. I remember thinking about it and feeling for the first time family pride welling within my small chest. One day, would I be called, 'Mr Lowe'?

I retrace the route we would then have followed, a giant of a man in a gaberdine mac and a flat cap and a skinny boy in shorts, down by the river the other way towards the reservoir, to tickle trout, or along to the allotments for a crack with the men.

14

I go into the pub early and sit with a pint of Robinson's mild because it's what my grandfather drank, and the paper, because that's what he did. The decor has changed, and the name. For all I know this is where he sat.

The barmaid – she may be the landlady – has an ample chest and a tight white blouse, a hairdo that cost fifty quid and too much gold on her ears. A thin old man in a suit and white socks – I take him to be a travelling salesman – sits on a barstool with a Special Brew and a packet of fags.

'I know your face,' he says, after a few minutes of sideways glances.

My heart goes into my boots, I had hoped that I could remain anonymous.

'Was your father Arthur Lowe?'

'Yes,' I say.

'Eeeeeee. He was a grand chap. Do you know . . . ' he takes a cigarette from the packet and taps it on the bar before putting it in his mouth and, eyes screwed up against the smoke, lights it. He addresses the barmaid, not me.

'Do you know, Arthur were Chairman of the Cricket Club for twenty-two years? He were a bloody cracking bloke, he were.' He stands up to go, doing up his jacket, fag bang in the middle of his mouth. He picks up a briefcase in his left hand and offers his right. It's thin and dry. Rather yellow, kind eyes look directly into mine.

'Y'know. You look just like him.'

He goes out through the door and the barmaid looks across at me and smiles, wrinkling her eyes and nose as if to say, 'Isn't that nice.'

I am, at one and the same time, relieved and irritated that the man has not got into a long discussion about

Swindley or Mainwaring, or asked me what I'm doing here. That he has skipped a whole generation, and mistaken me for my grandfather's son, I find hard to believe. Does he not watch television?

The instant dilution – like coffee granules – of two whole generations of Lowes poured away down the sink. It only takes a mouthful of alcohol these days to turn me morose. I go back out into the rain, two-thirds of a pint sitting on the hammered, lacquered, fake copper table.

When first I went to Hayfield as a young boy it was quite different; yellow-brown smoke hung over the cottage roofs from so many chimney stacks. One figure shutting his front door, the click of the Yale carrying across the silence, pulling up his collar and setting off down the steep main street.

At six every morning my grandfather came downstairs and polished his enormous leather shoes which were nearly boots. He never bought new ones, he got them repaired by a cobbler in a back street of Stockport. He wore grey socks and suspenders. Then he'd stoke the fire which he'd carefully banked up the night before. Nan would come down to the tiny kitchen and make tea, a bird-like woman flitting from kettle to pot. While she laid out breakfast my Grandad would do the rounds of several elderly neighbours to make sure they'd survived the night.

He didn't knock, he just walked in and shouted up the stairs.

'Are you OK? It's a right cold morning Mrs So-and-So.'

At breakfast he would check his half hunter by the pips on the wireless. 'I'll have to take this in and have it adjusted, it's running early again.'

The main employment was at the Ferodo brake linings factory, Froods in dialect. The neighbour Albert Jepsom worked there. It was very quiet in the village and when he stood at his open door and whistled a tune for the sheer joy of living you could hear him from down by the river. Albert and his wife Nellie were pioneers, along with Trevor the taxi, of the coach tour to Spain. Thirty jolly couples chyacking, singing Viva l'Espagna, having to stop the bus to relieve themselves.

There's a danger of painting them with too coarse a brush. In the main they were well-read, well-travelled, outward-looking people. Albert played brass band music very loud on the gramophone and together he and his beloved Nellie strode out for ten miles and more in the long summer evenings.

People met at The Railway or The George and on birthdays and anniversaries dined out at The Lamb. The fittings were a bit brassy and village folk were living very fast, eating coq au vin.

Half of them still went to church on a Sunday. Grandad had a fine baritone voice and loved to let rip in the hymns. He sang at The Railway sometimes too, until they told him to belt up.

On my early visits we arrived, like everybody else, by train. Grandad would meet us at the station and he'd carry one of the lighter bags because he had bronchitis. The result of mustard gas in the First War. Joanie, my mother, was never able to resist those suitcase offers in the colour supplements so we always had one suitcase which was much too big. It fell to Dad to carry it – if the porter could not be persuaded for a shilling to take it up to the cottage on his barrow. Red in the face, I can hear him say, 'What fool designed this?'

It was good to arrive like this, ordered. Later we arrived by car. Arthur had bought a 1948 Daimler drop-head coupé, HDK 351, and our arrivals were very grand and very late and accompanied by lengthy discussions as to which way we'd come. We should have come by Matlock, they'd widened it through there. But if we had come by Matlock then we should have stayed on the A515. The car had to be parked right outside the cottage at considerable inconvenience to the neighbours. At that tender age I was unaware of the concept 'local boy made good'.

The car was horribly unreliable, and the bonnet would be lifted. It hinged lengthways in two halves, and so-and-so's lad – who knew about cars – would come and tinker. It would then run quite reliably until we were just out of sight. Later it was found that the cylinder head was cracked which was why, if you walked off and left it for a bit and then went back, it would start again. Joan had some practical knowledge of cars. Her parents had lived over Kinder at Edale, and motoring, summer and winter, was an essential part of their lives. As a young girl she'd helped, with frozen fingers, to put on the chains for the steep climb out of the village.

On one occasion, with the car pulled over to the side of the road and the bonnet up, a short-trousered me kicking road chips into the ditch, Dad had just spent twenty minutes taking out the six sparking plugs, cleaning and drying them, setting the gaps and putting them back while Mum sat on the back seat with The Times crossword. Her voice wafted out through the open window, 'I expect the sparking plugs are dirty.'

They took the delays entirely in their stride and sometimes took three days from Manchester to London discovering delightful little hotels and charming people along the way.

Years later, when she was dying, we'd sit and drink gin together and play tapes. I'd put on Tom Waits and we'd listen to his gravel-in-a-bucket voice, 'It could be your carburettor, it could be your coil.' It reminded us of those happy, unpredictable days with Henry Daimler Knight 351.

Then the branch line closures came and for a while the village died. Many people had to move to Stockport or Cheadle so they could get to work, in winter it can snow for a week and even the gritters can't get through. The character of the main street changed to the way it is now as I look down it, blocked with cars. And when the dual carriageway came the village was split in half, physically and culturally. The cottage where Granny, Mary Annie Ford, was born is a restaurant now, so that's where I sit to eat my lunch. I pull a press cutting from my pocket, something I found in a drawer on the boat, it tells how Arthur Lowe (senior) and Mary Annie Ford were married on June 29th 1910 and had a Pretty Hayfield Wedding:

> PRETTY HAYFIELD WEDDING. – A very pretty wedding was solemnised at the Hayfield Parish Church on Wednesday afternoon, in which the parties concerned were Mr Arthur Lowe, eldest son of Mr T. Lowe, of Godley, and Miss Mary Annie Ford, only daughter of Mr Joe Ford, of Hayfield. The bride, who was given away by her father, was tastefully attired in a saxe blue costume, with Paris net blouse and hat to match; she also carried a pretty bouquet of

roses and carnations, the gift of the bridegroom. Her attendant maids were Miss J. Ford,
of Chapel-en-le-Frith (aunt of the bride), and
Miss M. Lowe (sister of the bridegroom). Miss
Ford wore a dress of cream and a black picture
hat, while Miss Lowe wore a saxe blue costume
and black picture hat. Each lady also carried
bouquets of lilies of the valley, the gifts of the
bridegroom. The duties of best man were
entrusted to Mr George Lowe, of Godley. The
nuptial ceremony was conducted by the Rev. W
Rickaby, after which about 60 guests sat down
to an excellent repast at the bride's home,
where dancing and singing were largely in-
dulged in. Mr and Mrs Lowe, who have been
the recipient of numerous useful presents, left
later in the day for Southport to spend the
honeymoon. They will afterwards take up their
residence at Oldham, where the bridegroom is
employed on the railway.

Little Arthur was born on 22 September 1915 which
almost certainly has something to do with big Arthur
going off to fight in the trenches in France. Young wives
relying only on a postcard for news of their husbands
were inclined to forget their douche.

Afterwards, when I've finished my chips, introspective
and haunted, I stroll over to the cottage where big
Arthur and Nan lived. Where they died. Where Joanie,
my mother, went to end her days, curled up on the floor
like a wounded animal, drunk and bleeding inside.
Telling the do-gooders to piss off. Cruelly snubbing old
Alice, her last friend. I peep in the windows, aware that

I may not want to see what meets my gaze, it belongs to someone else now. Family history traded for money in the bank, pragmatism ruling the heart, ghosts walking, yet to be laid. The curtains are drawn so the problem is resolved.

I can remember the interior as if I was standing there. I can smell the gas cooker and the coal in the bucket, grandfather's cheroot. Big Arthur never spoke of the First World War but he had some gruesome brass trophies converted to cigarette lighters and so on, balanced on the red brick fireplace. Every time he lit up I thought I could smell German blood. He was a tall man and must have been powerful in his day, an infantryman with a bayonet and muddied boots. The British Tommy.

He was in communion with nature's cycle. He loved a new season's Manx kipper. He knew all the best spots for mushrooms.

'I'd like it if you'd take me with you one day, Arthur,' said Mr Andrews to him once.

They walked thirteen miles, uphill and down dale, and they never saw a mushroom.

'It's a simple matter of deduction now, Mr Andrews.'

When big Arthur was in the bathroom shaving and little Arthur was in the bedroom and I was playing on the twisty stair, Nan would call up.

'Arthur!'

And they would both shout down.

'Yes, what?'

In old age big Arthur passed some of his time in The Lamb where he often earned his pints by telling unlikely yarns to hikers; he died when he was eighty-something. Nan died when she was ninety-nine, so she must have outlived her son by two years. I was drinking heavily by then and I'm ashamed to say I can't recall her passing.

Down by the cricket ground, which has meant so much to us all, an old tarpaulin is stretched across the wicket. The wind has come now and it flogs at its lashings. It has turned cold and I zip my jacket and wish that I'd bothered to put on socks. Half of me says I shouldn't have come, the other half says it's one necessary stage in a long process of healing.

To cheer myself I get the dashboard Christmas Tree from its box. The wires are still there from last year and I twist them together and the lights start winking, I lick the suction cup with a rather dry tongue and we're in business, it's well into December now. There's a tape of Christmas Carols too, so I put that on and drive off down the road to Jingle Bells.

2

'Keep it up lad, you're doing a grand job'
1915–1945

SOUTH Manchester isn't pretty. But then it probably never was. The locals say it's changed but what they really mean is that the people have changed. Most of the people on the street that I can see are Indian or Pakistani. Colourful, self-sufficient, happy, honourable people who – whatever anybody says – really belong wherever fate has washed them up. Any white faces are withered old ladies, hunched old men, Lowryesque, grotesque. Rubbish blows along the wide pavements and any fine facades that remain are obscured by illuminated plastic shop signs.

Between the wars the Lowes lived in Levenshulme. They had a house off the Lonsdale Road. Big Arthur worked at London Road Station and little Arthur went to Chapel Street Elementary, the 'Tin School'. His teachers there were Alberta Robson, Elizabeth Parry and Miss Crossley, who took French and also drama. Blessed Miss

Crossley who showed a little boy how he could do something. So that he could go on and learn how to do it well. Blessed be Miss Crossley. She had austere looks, a de Gaulle nose and an Eton crop.

Arthur did well at school, and his old chum from those days, Harold Grimshaw – alone now, the biggest thing in his day his lunch – remembers him playing the colonel in *The Grand Cham's Diamond*. Arthur had a gun and he pulled it out and shot him. They were boy scouts, and wags, and ladies' men from an early age. Arthur was keen on a girl called Mildred Nutall. I've tried to track her down but time has rubbed out her traces. Harold was seeing Joan Kiernan; the two boys used to go together to watch the girls playing basketball in their short skirts.

Then they were at Alma Park Central School, a secondary grammar. Arthur was a handy boxer and the boys used to meet in Fred Gort's basement where they'd improvised a ring. He was light on his feet and aggressive, hard to beat. At weekends and in the holidays they went to the Chalton Palais and danced to the music of Harry Roy, the girls gathered down one side, the boys down the other.

The family moved to the Barcicroft Road, and when he left school in 1931 Arthur got a job as a barrow boy for a cotton mill, pushing a handcart through the Manchester streets. Later he got a job at the Fairey Aviation Works at Heaton Chapel and at Brown Brothers, selling motor parts. Arthur Jarvis remembers him from those days, in a letter to me: 'Many were the laughs we had with him as he was very good at mimicking the foremen and various other bosses.'

I'm in an area called Rusholme now, dodging about in heavy traffic, stealing company diesel for my own magical mystery tour. I'm a bit beyond caring. I'm going to go and take a peek at the place where it could be said it all began, Leslie's Pavilion.

The stage began to play a part in Arthur's life around about when he was seventeen. He went with his mates – maybe with Mildred, who knows? – and paid sixpence to sit on benches and watch a concert party. If it was raining – not unusual in Manchester, it's pelting now, blowing brollies inside out – they could hardly hear the players for the cats and dogs on the tin roof. Harry Leslie, one of Rusholme's great characters, owned it. He was a talented ventriloquist and gave up employment at a cotton mill to bring showbusiness to the suburbs. He started in a marquee on the same site, a real eccentric and a real trier. I can't say that that, where that shop is now, is exactly where it was, can't pinpoint it. When I see the Birch Villa pub then I know I'm somewhere near. Leslie's Pavilion closed at the beginning of the war, and it was knocked down in the seventies. Dad would have have been drawn to a man like Harry Leslie like a can of spinach to a magnet. He admired entrepreneurs, impresarios, theatre managers, risk-takers, men who stood or fell by their own decisions. He loved people who were just a little larger than life itself.

Beryl Reid kicked off from here. She was working as a shop assistant at Kendal Milne's, the fancy Manchester store, desperate to get on the stage. In her lunch time she shot through to Leslie's Pavilion to audition for Fred Rayne. She'd devised a little act in which she was a hotel maid cleaning shoes. When she'd cleaned the shoes she impersonated the owners; she got a job at two quid a week playing Bridlington.

Arthur's father and mother were very fond of Music

Hall. Young Arthur often went with them, and so his next experience of the stage was at the Bertie Crewe-designed Manchester Palace of Varieties. There I suppose he'd have seen artists like Gracie Fields, Elsie and Doris Waters, Tommy Handley and Will Hay. He applied for a scene shifter's job (his father's duties at the railway company included making the travel arrangements for touring companies, and he gave his son the necessary introduction), and Arthur, sober and good at organising, was made up to an assistant stage manager. There can be no doubt that he stood in the wings night after night and watched, among others, Will Hay and Robb Wilton: both artists to whom his own style has been attributed. The trend was towards drama and away from variety. He's thought to have had some walk-on parts but there's no record of them.

Harold Grimshaw last saw Arthur in 1938, he was standing on the corner of Cringle Road and Heaton Moor Road waiting for a tram to Stockport. As if anticipating some future role, he was wearing a black overcoat and a bowler hat and carrying a rolled umbrella. I go around there and park up, I watch for a while but I can't see him, there's too many living people getting in the way.

1938? Things were hotting up in Europe. Boys of Arthur's age listened to the wireless and watched for the headlines on the news stands. Arthur's father, remembering his fallen comrades on the Somme, said he felt no pride, just dread, when Arthur joined the Duke of Lancaster's Own Yeomanry. They were a cavalry regiment: the local gentry were its officers, the local lads its men. They were booted and spurred with chain-mail vests and bearing musket and sword. The cold steel.

The headline of the Daily Mirror on Monday September 4th 1939 confirmed big Arthur's – and everybody's – fears: BRITAIN'S FIRST DAY OF WAR: CHURCHILL IS NEW NAVY CHIEF.

It's been said that a strange silence hung over the City. The King's words rang in the air.

'The task will be hard. There may be dark days ahead . . . But we can only do the right as we see the right, and reverently commit our cause to God. If one and all we keep resolutely faithful to it, ready for whatever service or sacrifice it may demand, then, with God's help, we shall prevail.'

The Duke of Lancaster's Own Yeomanry had been called to full-time war service three days before, on 1 September, and Arthur Lowe's real war had begun.

I drive back to the cinder yard ready for the morning. I eat some cheese that I have left over and get into my bunk early. There's half a bottle of the brown drink, the stuff of dreams. I wake in the small hours and try to think what it must have been like for him, for them. The boys were billeted in a rat infested cotton mill with no proper bedding and nothing but square-bashing to pass the days. Ripped from their villages, and awaiting they knew not what.

Several survivors from this time have told me about Von Kramm, the imaginary Nazi officer whose character Arthur developed during the long, cold days and nights at Hawkshaw. 'Velcome to my vawr.' A ripple of laughter goes round. A disembodied Mancunian voice comes out from under a blanket.

'Belt up, Arthur, can't you?'

'My name is Colonel Von Kramm and it is I who vill be asking ze qvestions.'

The disembodied voice becomes carnate in the form of Mr Chuckles of Lancashire Chlorides.

'Hitch up, driver. You're next.'

Men in blue overalls and flat caps, driving yellow fork-lift trucks, start putting black drums of something very nasty onto the trailer and their voices carry across the morning.

Arthur saved himself from going mad by listening to the voices around him, his messmates, the officers, Sergeant Jack Ashworth. Rehearsing in private and then trotting out such perfect mimicry that he could have the troop leaping to attention by their beds before jumping on him and ragging him. He got quite a reputation amongst his mates – Ernest Skidmore, Dick Willows – as a practical joker. Tom Walklett recalls Arthur calling out in the voice of one of their officers, 'Sergeant Ashworth to the Squadron Office, please!' When the hapless Sergeant doubled round to the Squadron Office there was Arthur. Alone. 'No, no officers here. Just me, Sergeant.'

A lading slip is shoved through the window for me to sign, I keep my copy. Chains and ropes and canvas occupy my hands for half an hour then I'm off down the road, black smoke this time, and using every gear up into the red band. Two thousand kilometres of open road await me and it's like Doctor Brighton blowing in through an open window in summer.

*

They requisitioned horses from the pony club, from haulage contractors and dairies. They had a Vickers gun on a carriage and when the gun was to be readied for action the soldier shouted, 'Milko!' and the horse

28

dutifully came to a halt. Arthur was assigned a small horse called Daisy. He wrote regularly to the lady owner, reassuring her:

> . . . I'm sure we won't be taking the horses into action. It seems more likely we will be attached to mechanised units . . .

They had fifty-seven bits of brass to polish on their uniforms, and a sword to burnish. Brass buckles on the saddlery and all the tack had to be done with saddle soap. There wasn't just white blanco, there was russet blanco, and green blanco too. There was black boot-polish and the officer inspecting wore white gloves which he wiped around the horses' docks in case there was a trace of anything brown.

The D.L.O.s requisitioned civilian vehicles too, driving around in a lorry with 'Persil' on the headboard and an old furniture van with 'W.H.Evans' on its canvas tilt. Arthur was put in charge of the M.T. Office where his job was issuing worksheets to the drivers. At Pembroke Dock they defended the harbour with one Lewis gun and a 6" Howitzer with wooden wheels and a plate on it which said 'Birmingham Parks'.

It might be a comic scene, muddled up in my head with *Dad's Army*, but a cello has begun its sinister song. War brings chilling images to the surface: mass troop movements, evacuation, bombed out houses, I've only ever seen it on telly. This was to be a modern war, they said, soon to be over, not a war for horses, but I see him in black and white, slightly undercranked, a scratch running down one side of the frame, a straight-backed hussar on a black horse, behind him a pair of matched stallions pulling a gun-carriage. The dead lie in the ditches on the side of the rough road and he turns to look back down the column, standing in the saddle. It isn't Arthur of course. It's some old footage I saw and got confused.

Soon the regiment was, as they had predicted, attached to the Royal Artillery. The laughing boys were moved from Pembroke Dock to Pontypridd, then to Market Hill in Northern Ireland. They were cold, poorly quartered and bored. Thoughts turned inward and even Von Kramm fell silent, pre-occupied with the awful progress of the war.

Arthur was now a clerk and had risen to the rank of Corporal. Bill Bateman ran a little danceband, 'The Jive Five', but Arthur wouldn't join. I can hear him – with Mainwaring's voice – chiding.

'This is no time for jiving.'

I suppose he didn't speak like that then. He spoke with a slight Lancashire accent, one might reasonably guess that his voice then was quite light, compared to the voice we all remember now. He was described to me as pompous by an old comrade, then Private Tomlinson, who remembers him in his elevated position of clerk in the battery office at Gosford Castle. And Nobby Hewitt says he used to go about the business of the day quietly imitating the danceband crooners. I remember Dad saying he used to put a row of pens in his battledress top pocket because their officer thought one pen was smart but more was unsoldierly. When I watch the start of the *Dad's Army* film – which I do quite often – I note that Pike gets told off about the pens in his top pocket. I bet that's a bit of business Arthur devised.

*

The road is clear and I get to Portsmouth in good time, the customs papers are with the agent and I'm booked on. There's a lot of shunting of heavy trucks, triple axles graunching as they are dragged this way and that. There's a lady driver shipping out tonight and her blonde curls are the only kind thing in this harsh scene, the cutting edge of commerce. A huge crash accompanies my trailer's wheels hitting the loading ramp and the sound echoes in the cavernous hold of the ship. The crew come with the securing chains even as I climb down. Just after eleven we're steaming out past the Battery, the gale has passed and the wind is in the North West and falling light. To the gentle lift in the sea I have time to dream again.

*

In 1942 he was successful in getting an attachment to REME to work on the new invention, radar. Once a journalist reported that he had attended RADA, but she misreported it. What in fact had been said was that, during the war, Arthur attended to radar.

And while attending to radar and other electromechanical things, he studied the people around him. He was what has come to be called a student of human nature. Later that year he went to the Middle East in the 'Queen Mary'.

The outward voyage in the 'Mary' made a great impression on Arthur, he reminisced about it often. The great liners down to the most pathetic rusty coaster stirred his blood. He held precious a romantic image in his mind's eye of the stoical, calculating Captain pitting his wits against the forces of nature. Judging the run of the tide. Dealing mischievously with bent port agents. Being father to his men. He held a love of the sea, or rather a love of his vision of the sea, close to his heart all his life. He nearly burst with pride when I joined Ellerman City Line, knew total despair when I left. He would most certainly have followed the sea himself but for his eyesight. He read the *Captain Kettle* stories as a boy and saw the deep-sea ships towing up the Manchester Ship Canal to the wharves at Salford. When his work in television brought him the wherewithal he bought himself a copper-bottomed boat. But more of that later.

Harold had last seen him in 1938 dressed for all the world like a bank manager, Bill in 1942 when they received their postings, now I had lost the scent. Then they did a piece in the Mail, and before long Norman Littlechild wrote to me. Norman had been with Arthur in the desert, and he had a playbill which he very kindly sent me. It was a strange handpainted playbill for *The Monkey's Paw*, put on by REME No.1 Welfare Club. The colours were blood red and violet, it had been folded, and the creases were set into the flimsy paper. It had an aura. And there was the author W.W.Jacobs staring at me off the page, making me wonder who chose the play. A month passed while I photographed it and reproduced it as a poster. I sent Norman a copy, and he in turn sent me a tape on which he'd recorded some anecdotes, precious memories shared.

Norman had met Arthur on the edge of the Sinai Desert at Rafah. They were in the REME unit called the 15th Radio Repair Workshops. They were guarding a big ordnance depot, living under canvas – it became one of Arthur's recurring phrases, 'we were living under canvas you know' — and their job was to repair and maintain the ack-ack and searchlight radars. They were in amongst high sand dunes and nearby were the old Turkish lines from the First War. Everything there, just about, was made of wood and hessian. Mock aeroplanes, mock depots, mock guns. Men were detailed just to walk back and forth to the mock latrines.

High up in the sky German reconnaissance crews probably said to one another,

'Ze Tommy can never vin zis vawr, he is alvays running to ze little house!'

Watch out though boys, because some of the guns were real, and this kind of elaborate ploy, crazy as it might seem, was one of the ways in which we did win the war.

> The only form of entertainment was an open-air cinema. You couldn't go to that every night and you couldn't get pissed every night, so, since some of the chaps were sand-happy and there was nothing else to do, I hit on the idea of doing a play. I don't know why because I'd had no experience apart from acting in plays at school.
> *Arthur Lowe quoted in Richard Fawkes' book,*
> *'Fighting For A Laugh'*

One day on the notice board in the NAAFI Norman saw a note which had been posted by Arthur suggesting the formation of an amateur dramatics group. The two soldiers joined forces, encouraged their mates, and soon a strong troupe had been formed. A REME unit was ideal for a venture like this because they had access to every trade and a wealth of engineering resource at their disposal. A stage was built, lights and scenery. *The Monkey's Paw* was their first production, the playbill Norman had sent me. There was the part of Mrs White, played by Welshman Thomas Thomas, and a wig was needed. Someone made one from cotton wool. Once rigged with the wig, the Welshman became quite fanciable!

Another chap who had got close with Arthur was Chalky White. He remembers the NAAFI theatre as being already in place and Arthur getting permission to use it. They were called 'The Pilgrim Players' and Chalky made the props and helped build the sets. In their second production, *Recall,* Chalky played the part of the Batman. An Indian – he's not sure how he came to be there – sat cross-legged at the back and played the pipes. One night Arthur broke his dentures, eating a goat sandwich, and had to do the performance with his top set held together with chewing gum.

The boys made their own wireless sets in the workshops and would listen to the news from home. They'd take it down, and then Arthur would sit in the NAAFI and read it out, the perfect rip-off of Winston Churchill. They had a dinner gong on which they struck the chimes of Big Ben.

Norman and Arthur took a leave together in Jerusalem. They had to run the gauntlet of a pack of slavering dogs in the village to catch the night train. They sat in the Garden of Gesthemane like regular tourists and took tea at cafés. One little thing sticks in Norman's mind – a waiter had just brought a tray out to their table and Arthur's cup was cracked. When he complained the waiter shrugged. Arthur smashed the cup on the table – he could get very shirty if everything wasn't just right.

Arthur had an affinity with Jews and Arabs alike. He could even look Jewish in a certain light, and it was one of his disguises when we lived at Little Venice. He'd set off for the deli wearing the complete regalia, apparently unrecognisable. But while he browsed the shelves our neighbour – a big, gentle man from Maine, something in the music business, in for pastrami and bagels – would put his head down to Arthur's ear and whisper,

'Morning, Arthur.'

Arthur would hold his hand up to his mouth in that little way he had and say,

'How did you know?'

He spoke near fluent Arabic – one day outside Harrods an Arab who was making a beeline for the open door of his stretched Mercedes paused for an instant, recognition flickering across his face as he saw Arthur. They exchanged the usual greeting. 'Salam alaikum.' Then they conversed for a moment in Arabic. Who was he? I asked as we walked along towards home.

'Don't know the man from Adam,' Dad replied.

That mysterious Tintin-style meeting stayed with me for years, playing on my mind. Only later did I realise that even Arab Sheiks, or anyway their wives, watch *Coronation Street*.

But the rumour that he was in the Camel Corps was one he started and nurtured himself. Norman says he saw him on a horse once, galloping across the desert, a romantic figure standing in the saddle, kicking up a cloud of dust.

They were rehearsing *Bound East For Cardiff*, by Eugene O'Neill, when they actually had to go and do something for the war effort. They started loading into trucks. There was a Scotch officer who had spent his war collecting stones: even in this emergency, he was seen trying to reserve some space on the truck for his crates. It must have taken people different ways: the heat, and the excruciating boredom.

They drove down dangerous desert roads to Haifa and when they got there put on a revue. Arthur had written a book – a novella about a soldier who was posted missing or something – but when he showed it to their C.O. he didn't think much of it. Arthur was a bit down in the dumps. He was going to try and join ENSA when last Norman saw him. Chalky and Arthur stayed together a bit longer. They, with the rest of the 8th Army, were outside Tobruk when they parted.

A new adventure was awaiting Arthur:

> When Torin Thatcher asked if I would like to join his new units I said, yes, I would. What we did was to form a unit with an officer, a senior NCO, an NCO, a driver and a spare hand, and our job was to go out to lonely places in the desert and help them put on their shows.
>
> We weren't allowed to play ourselves, just help produce, stage manage or give them tips on how to build scenery. Since by this time there was a fair amount of stuff available in Cairo, if they wanted to start a small band, we could even provide them with instruments.
>
> *Arthur Lowe in 'Fighting For A Laugh'*

These Units – extremely mobile and operating independently – were used for intelligence gathering, and it may be that Arthur, with his command of Arabic, was engaged in this sort of work. More than one old comrade thinks so. The desert life suited Arthur, he was lean and hard. His blue eyes were very bright in his cheeky brown face. I wish I could have known him then.

With the progression of the war the brief was changing, and now Arthur and Martin Benson opened a fortnightly rep above the Pay Corps office in Alexandria. Benson was already established as an actor and after the war he had an extensive film career, spanning forty years. They called their theatre the Mercury. I found this newspaper cutting:

NEW FORCES THEATRE OPENS IN ALEX

The No. 2 Field Entertainment Unit has created the Mercury Theatre, Alex., and it is obvious that it has the equipment, personal and technical, to provide the city, and particularly the forces stationed in the area, with first class plays. The Unit chose for its opening production *Without The Prince*, a comedy centring round the attempt of country amateurs to put on *Hamlet*, and a case of lost memory. Everything depends on the Stranger whose memory has deserted him, and in this the producer, Arthur Lowe, was well served by Neil Wilson. As the slightly guilty stranger, as the Prince, and as the West End star, he was equally convincing.

A performance in many ways remarkable was given by Audrey Simms, as the country Ophelia. She holds her audience with ease and confidence, but she must learn to hold her interpretation even when she is in the background. Ted Byford's acting as the farmer steadily improved and in the third act he was one of the marked successes. Vance Rotheram, his son, has obvious acting ability, but his performance lacked consistency. In a small part at the end of the play, Julien Brownhill was decorative and effective.

One or two of the actors were called upon to play parts for which their age disqualified them, but we felt that without this handicap June Theophilus and Norman Guilmant might do well.

Martin Benson, who directs the theatre, has achieved a marvel of organisation in the short space of six weeks, and Arthur Lowe has put on a play which will certainly give much needed entertainment to the Services and their friends. Our one real grouse is that this ought to have been done a long time ago. – D.D.H.

In another production, Anne Pringle, Anne Ferguson WRNS then, remembers Martin Benson in rehearsal sitting at the back of the stalls and shouting at her as she moved woodenly around the stage, trying her best. She says he wasn't very popular. Arthur, now promoted to the rank of Sergeant, was directing as well as playing. In 1965 an old comrade from that time, Ernest Helmwood, wrote to Arthur:

'Keep It Up Lad, You're Doing A Grand Job!'
I wonder how many times you made this remark during your stay at the Mercury Theatre in Alexandria? On the receiving end were such characters as Neil Wilson; Henry Manning; Nick Noon; Ted Byford; etc., etc.

I recall Martin Benson wandering around the place like a lost soul – no doubt wondering what he had done to deserve being lumbered with such a team. Nevertheless they were happy days for me, and I, for one, very thoroughly enjoyed myself at the Mercury.

Shortly after the war Martin Benson was kind enough to offer me the position of S/M at the Arts Theatre in London but, for a number of reasons, I was unable to accept. I did stand-in backstage to assist Torin Thatcher at the Westminster Theatre on one occasion and Neil Wilson was also there – in civilian clothes and not police uniform, which made a change!

I am enclosing a couple of mementos of the Mercury Theatre which may prove of interest to you. The photograph reminds me that on the last performance of *Thunder Rock* poor old Nick Noon REALLY staggered with those parcels. Some clot had filled the can; bunged bricks and stones in the box; and well-weighted the interior of the radio set! Was it you?

If you have a few minutes to spare I'd very much appreciate a few lines from you and, if ever you are in this delightful vicinity, do please drop in. You can be very certain of a really warm welcome.

Keep it up OLD lad – you're doing a great job!

Neil Wilson was to become my Godfather, though it was only when I started writing this book that I realised how he and Arthur had first met. They were doing a revue, *Button Sticks And Bull,* when the war hotted up a bit.

Bill Pilkington arrived at the theatre one night – a big mock front-of-house had been erected – to find it dark. He asked who was in charge.

'The Director's a REME chap, Arthur Lowe, God knows where he is at the moment, there's been a hell of a lot of movement of troops, but he seems to be the Brain.'

Bill, who had missed Arthur twice now – the first time being at the Royal College of Languages in Beirut, interesting snippet, that one – finally met up with him further up the line. The thing which struck him at that meeting was the detail Arthur held in his head. For the Mercury Theatre and for future productions. He felt he had a very sharp mind.

Arthur was demobbed in January 1946. A thin British Sergeant in a demob suit and his army boots, frozen to the bone on a railway station, like a million others looking to pick up the threads of their pre-war lives. Relieved to be home but uncertain of employment, emotionally unsettled, no longer able to find satisfaction in the humdrum.

3

'A vice-like grip on Monday's sparse attendance'

1923–1961

I SHOULD tell you about my mother now, because she has more bearing on the story of my father's career than you might at first credit. Theirs is an extraordinary love story.

Joan Cooper was born in Chesterfield on 10 August 1923. Her father was organist and choirmaster there, her mother a contralto.

She learnt the piano – the old method, rapped over the knuckles until you got it right – and might have been expected to follow a career in music like her parents. However she preferred the stage, and so, at fifteen, she went to join the Stratford-upon-Avon Dramatic School.

At seventeen she joined the ranks of Donald Wolfit's company and in my child's eye I see her in a hat at train call. When I pass through Derby, on the train North, as I do now about once a month, I sometimes think I see her. She played for Randall Ayrton too. Later she joined the Colchester Repertory Company where she worked her way up to stage manager and played occasional parts as well. By the outbreak of the war she'd married a Canadian actor, Richard Gatehouse. Ritchie came from a family of sailors – his brothers were back home running the ferry somewhere – and was RNVR, Royal Navy Volunteer Reserve, the Wavy Navy. They had a son David, and a girl Jane, but she died while still a baby.

With Ritchie away at sea Joan worked at the little theatre at Farnham, a converted 16th-century barn. The resident staff was just two girls. I went there with her once, it was a lovely theatre and I could see she missed it terribly. At that age I couldn't know just how deep her feelings were running.

I was only a child when she told me about her wartime experiences, and it seems I am the only person she ever related them to, so they are a little muddled. She told me about falling from a tram in the black-out in Colchester, of being helped to her feet by a man who wanted to take advantage of her, of being strafed by a low-flying aircraft while crossing a park, seeing the bullets hitting the grass. She used to choose not to go down to the air-raid shelters but trusted to her luck and kept her dignity in the rooms where she stayed. She said she would turn the wireless up to drown out the sounds around her. There's a photograph of her on this newspaper cutting I have in front of me while I write. She really does look a dame. But I'm going to put it aside and move on because it's making me cry.

She was impressed by the Americans – mainly by their trousers – with their brash good humour and their chocolate but she said she never took one as a lover.

42

Ritchie, with a commission now, was posted to the Shetlands. The Norwegians were active with their fishing boats running agents into occupied Norway, and these brave men, who dared the winter storms for the cover they afforded, were so reliable they came to be called the Shetland Bus. The agents used to get nailed up in false bulkheads in case the Germans put a search party aboard. Ritchie's job was to go out in a little launch and meet these boats and others as they approached the shore to check their credentials.

The couple and their young son lodged with Grace Thompson, who sat by the fire and knitted Shetland jumpers, two a week. My mother always longed to return there, and when Arthur died I thought for a while she would. She had a vision of it as a land of plenty and compassion.

Modern communications hadn't reached to the islands then, and the way of life was simple and self-sufficient, a style that suited her. David, her little boy, was well provided for as eggs, butter, fish and potatoes were in plentiful supply in the islands, and Grace was a source of unquestioned wisdom as to the needs of a child. The real war was a long way off. In winter the gales lashed Scalloway, and there were days when no-one could leave their cottages for being blown clean away. I don't know when (David was knocked off his bicycle when he was eleven and can remember nothing before that age, so he's no help) but sometime before 1948 Ritchie and Joan Gatehouse returned to England, to resume their theatre careers. Their relationship fell to bits after this, the turmoil of wartime life must have upset many people this way, and Joan joined Frank H. Fortescue's company alone.

It was on a crowded post-war train, a thousand displaced persons jostling in the smoke-filled corridors all looking to their homes, that Joan met the frozen sergeant. She was going to Manchester to play the Hulme Hippodrome. He was going home, perhaps to take up his old job at Fairey Aviation, perhaps not. He thought she was very good-looking, vivacious, an actress. She thought he was an amusing, intense man, in need of warmth.

Drawn to the girl he had met on the train, and banking on the experience of dramatics he had gained in the desert, Arthur prevailed upon his father again to give him the introduction he needed.

Theatre companies at that time hired a whole train to transport the cast, stage-management, scenery and props – the 'train call' early on a Sunday morning was all part of the fun for touring players – and big Arthur, who booked these trains for the managements, was well-known to Fortescue. The company was badly in need of male actors (bitter fact of war, that) and Arthur got an audition. He had a lot going for him. He was slightly short, bald and wore glasses. He was never going to be offered the male lead, but he was the perfect all-purpose recipe for character parts. It doesn't do to be taller than the leading man, especially if he's only five feet nine in lifts, and a bald pate takes a hairpiece like nothing else.

Arthur told me once about Frank H. Fortescue. It seems he was a larger-than-life character, even viewed in the half-light of time. He had started in the theatre at the age of fourteen performing a different play every day in portable theatres and by the time he set up his own touring rep in 1914 it is said he had played every theatre in the country. A Brummy, he was as kind as he was tough. At the time Arthur got his audition, 'Oppy' – he got his by-name from his eternal optimism – was an impresario of substance, with successful companies in most cities.

So Arthur was signed on as one of THE FRANK H. FORTESCUE FAMOUS PLAYERS and unknown to himself or those around him had just put his foot on the first rung of a ladder that would take him to the top of his chosen profession. The theatre where he was going to play for the next year had first opened in 1901 as The Grand Junction Theatre owned by Broadhead. In 1905 it switched identities with the Hippodrome and Floral Hall. When Arthur came to it, it was also known as the Manchester Repertory Theatre, though, confusingly, the Manchester Repertory Company seems to have occupied another theatre further down the road.

His first appearance had been an isolated one in the November of 1945 playing the part of Dickson in *Bedtime Story*. Fortescue, and big Arthur, were in the front of house that night, at least until the interval. It seems Arthur gave a satisfactory performance because a message was sent round to the stage door from the pub saying he could start on a regular basis in the New Year. Joan was still married to Ritchie and trying to make a go of it, David was with his granny in Hexham during the school term and with his mother during the holidays. Arthur went home to his parents for Christmas, the first time for many years and the last – he never again had the time.

Nan wished Arthur would marry a local girl, though she had no one in particular lined up. Chesterfield was hardly the far side of the moon, but Nan couldn't take this in because Joan had been at drama school and spoke and behaved in a way quite alien to her. Divorce was not an easy pill for Nan to swallow either, and though she eventually got used to Joan there was never any love lost between the two. Big Arthur thought his boy should give the theatre a go, but not lose touch with his mates at Fairey's, keep his ear to the ground. With respect to Joan he felt that life was for living; he'd fought for that thirty years before. He used to give her hugs and blow his nose into a big handkerchief at their partings.

Just across from Manchester Central Station was Cox's Bar, there was a list of 'artists wanted' kept by the landlord, and, of the five theatres out along Oxford Street, four of them belonged to Frank H. Fortescue. Once in, there was no problem getting work. From January 1946 Arthur was appearing every week.

Terence Rattigan's *Flare Path* was the first play of that season, a piece about a test pilot, and I know it held a special place in Arthur and Joanie's hearts because from now on they started seeing each other on a regular basis.

They were in Manchester for exactly a year then left for Hereford to join Derek Salberg's company, Joan as stage manager. Here Arthur appeared in forty-two plays in a year, nothing unusual for a repertory actor. At Hereford, Arthur met again with Martin Benson. Mr Benson was directing and appearing; I don't know if that is how Arthur got the work down there, quite possibly. When I spoke with Derek Salberg on the phone ('Arthur never knew his lines, you know') he wasn't aware – thought I hadn't got it right – that Arthur and Martin Benson had met in North Africa. Salberg himself had been with Benson in Italy.

The first review I have, from the Hereford Times, is dated 15 January 1947. Arthur played Dr Brodman in Noël Coward's *Blithe Spirit*. First night fumbles marred an otherwise excellent production. The next week *Pink String And Sealing Wax* didn't open until the Tuesday because of the Film Society's show on the Monday. It gives a little insight into what rep was, then.

On February 5th the local hack reports them appearing in the Ibsen play, *Ghosts*:

> Opinions may differ as to whether *Ghosts* was a judicious choice for the first serious play to be done by the County Theatre Repertory Company, but as to the manner in which it is produced there can be only one opinion – that it rises well above the heights that could reasonably be expected even of Derek Salberg's ladies and gentlemen . . .
>
> Those who know their Ibsen will revel in each of the characterisations – Gerald Cuff as Pastor Manders, Beryl Johnstone as Mrs Alving, Leslie Yeo as Oswald, Helen Uttley as Regina Engstrand and Arthur Lowe as Engstrand. All five get the most out of their meaty parts, and the many emotional scenes, in which subdued fighting is employed with great effect, had a vice-like grip on Monday's sparse attendance.

The players continued the season with *Worm's Eye View* by R.F. Delderfield, Emlyn Williams's *The Corn Is Green, This Land Of Ours* by Lionel Brown, and another Coward, *This Happy Breed*. This time, in the paper, there's something which I notice:

> . . . and Arthur Lowe, as Frank Gibbon's crony gave the natural performance that one has come to expect of him.

During their time at Hereford, Joan and Arthur made many friends. Enduring friends whose names crop up again much later in their lives. When Joan got very poorly, towards the end of her life, she spoke more of the time at Hereford than of any other.

The last play that Arthur did for Derek Salberg at Hereford was *The Ghost Train* by Arnold Ridley. Amusing, that, when you think what would come later.

After Hereford they joined the company at Penge and Croydon with Reggie Salberg, Derek Salberg's brother, before heading for London in 1948. Just towards the end of that time Joan, who had been stage managing and sometimes appearing too, had miscarried and was not at all well. Miscarriage was what we call it in polite company, but she told me once that gin and a hot bath had brought it on quicker than lifting scenery. A child at that time in their lives would have been a disaster, and she wasn't ready to face the responsibility, the death of Jane still very large in her mind.

They were leaving behind the carefree part of their lives. Thinking back for a minute to what had gone before: they had come together by chance not a few miles from their respective homes having had experience of war and the theatre, one on the Home Front at Stratford and in Shetland, one in the desert of North Africa on makeshift stages. By the time Arthur came to London he had played in more than seventy plays and in some of them – like *The O'Mara Mystery* – he had played more than one part. It had been an apprenticeship which a young actor couldn't hope to have today with the passing of the rep companies, and the ennui of peacetime, and the high expectations we have set for our standard of living. Typically at that time he earned

£3 a week and of that £1 was paid out in rent and another £1 on a simple diet.

Joan Gatehouse, formerly Cooper, aged 25, married Arthur Lowe, aged 32, at Robert Adam Street Registry Office just off the Strand in London on 10 January 1948. They had no guests and they went out into the street and found two strangers, J.B. Hobbs and S. Barton, to be their witnesses. After they'd signed the register they went to a Lyon's Corner House for their tea. They had welsh rarebit, and I know that because whenever they wanted to remember that day in later years Joanie made them welsh rarebit. And after Arthur died Joan never ate it again. They took a room with friends at No. 10 Trevor Street, on the Knightsbridge side of Hyde Park.

For the next fourteen years Arthur was to work away unseen by the standards we apply to him today. He acted as his own agent and maintained a relentless bombardment on managements over the telephone. He is said to have been tireless and utterly persistent.

> I travelled a lot, took everything that was going, played whatever had to be played. How can you say you're an actor if you're not acting? An actor who can't support his family shouldn't be an actor. There's nothing so special about being an actor, nothing which allows you to be out of work more often than a bus-driver.
>
> *Interview with Sheridan Morley, The Times, 1974*

He traded higher billing for lower fee wherever he could and played the New Theatre, Bromley, which was so far away on the dreary Kent line that it barely paid at all. He earned, usually, £12 a week. If Bromley didn't have a part for him he'd get off the train at Penge and Croydon and ask there.

Arthur and Joan lived on next-to-nothing but never lost sight of the success that might lie ahead. Joan had great faith in Arthur's unique talent, and he in turn never let her down. She used to put the teacosy on the telephone to keep it warm and talk to Mr Lee, a little china Chinaman who stood – inscrutable, just as you might wish – on the mantelpiece. There was a bit of radio work, *Mrs Dale's Diary*, some commentaries for British Films. Joanie had sporadic work as assistant stage manager at the Arts. It didn't seem to be going anywhere much beyond Bromley. Arthur had promised himself five years to make a real go of it in the theatre or else he'd return to Manchester to take up work at Faireys or Ferodo. Joan would happily have starved before she saw him do that.

I realise I know little of my parents' early days in rep. I read hungrily through Henry Livings' *Rough Side Of The Boards* and Richard Jerrams *Weekly Rep.*

Richard Jerrams quotes Diane Glyn:

'Often we would have five or six changes of costume all provided by us and nothing could be worn again in a different play. I provided twenty full-length evening dresses, thirty-odd smart afternoon and cocktail dresses, had a dozen coats and skirts, negligées, stage undies, shoes.'

Each week they would perform that week's play, each evening plus matinées, and in the mornings they rehearsed next week's production, built, painted and lit the sets, gathered the props and made or altered their costumes. They worked at this pace with a tremendous tradition behind them and with financial insecurity in front of them, but always with a troupe of like-minded companions sharing the burden of the work and the chaotic first nights.

Henry Livings writes of himself in the third person:

' . . . What with emptying the dustbin, collecting props, prompting, scene setting and striking, making the calls front of house and backstage and making tea, he needed to be a quick study. Reg taught him make-up. A basic undercoat of Leichner's No.5 . . . '

Is it a wonder that hysterical laughter is associated with the theatrical profession? And now I begin to understand why Joanie needed the rhythm of the floor buffer during her long night vigils at Pavilion Road, when Arthur was away at Granada Television. She must have been as bored and as lonely as hell.

In the fifteen years between 1946 and 1961, which was when Arthur returned to Manchester to start on *Coronation Street,* he did a quite extraordinary quantity and diversity of work.

In 1947 he appeared in forty-two plays at the New Theatre Bromley. Amongst them was *Flare Path,* the play that meant so much to him and Joan, and many others whose titles are known to all of us, like *Blithe Spirit, Arsenic And Old Lace, The Ghost Train.* In 1948 he played Crabtree in *School For Scandal* for Basil Dean, while on radio he did *Mrs Dale's Diary* and something thrillingly titled *Adventure Unlimited.* That year, he made his first film appearances: as a man on the tube in *London Belongs To Me* and as a pianist in *Flood Tide.* He could play the piano a little, in a dance-band style, but living with Joan – who was quite a good pianist when she kept up her practice – he gave it up as a bad job. 1949 saw him back in rep at Croydon and Bromley but he managed to do more radio drama and more films. He had a good part as the reporter in *Kind Hearts And Coronets*. They still show it on the television, and it's marvellous to see how Arthur squeezes every drop out of a sound part and somehow makes it special. I switched on by chance in the last ten minutes of it just a few weeks ago. It was the last thing I watched before going to sleep that night. It had such a profound effect on me, he was still there when I woke in the morning.

All through 1950 he slogged away at Bromley, appearing in another twenty-eight plays. In 1951 he did the same but it was relieved by an isolated appearance at the Duke of York's Theatre in *Larger Than Life*. It was a comedy by Guy Bolton based on the novel *Theatre* by Somerset Maugham. Jack Minster directed and Arthur played the part of Wilson. It was his West-End debut, 7 February 1951. Joanie sent him a telegram: I HAVE BEEN SINGING OUR TUNE ALL MY LOVE = JOAN +++

He made his first television appearance that year too, for the record. It was something called *I Made News: Big Band*. That's the entry in Arthur's own notebook. The one he kept from that first appearance at Hulme Hippodrome back in 1945. And right up to the last entry on 13 March 1982 – exactly a month before he died – *Looks Familiar* for Thames. He didn't keep the book like a skite book. It was just so that he could check that he'd been paid.

From April 1950, he did commercial work, commentaries, voice-overs and so on. From his first commentary for Associated British Pathé to when he started on *The Street* he did thirty-six of these jobs advertising products as diverse as Wrigley's chewing gum, Black and Decker tools, Horlicks, Bisto and doing the voice-over for Pearl &

Dean cinema advertising films and a feature called *Shopping With The Stars*. You may recall the Wrigley's 'concentration' campaign: 'Speeds up to ninety, signals to watch . . . I find chewing Wrigley's Spearmint gum helps me to concentrate . . . ' Arthur's voice to the rhythm of the train.

Then in 1952 it came. Arthur's big chance. He was called to audition for the part of Senator Brockbank in *Call Me Madam*. At last – and not before time – a real break was in sight. The requirement was, of course, for an actor who could sing and dance.

Arthur had no trouble dancing, he was a good dancer. As a boy he had watched and imitated The Champion Clog Dancer Of The World. In Fred Gort's basement he had boxed. At the Chalton and Levenshulme Palais he'd not been slow in asking the girls up onto the floor – but sing? Yes, he'd mimicked the crooners but he'd never really had to sing before. Joan taught him 'Bye, Bye, Blackbird'. They worked hard at it, and when he left for the audition – a bag of nerves, for Arthur suffered stage-fright as badly as any other – he was good. He got the job.

He went to Frank Cooper's wine shop on the Brompton Road, just on the corner of the little mews Cheval Place, and bought a celebratory bottle of wine. Mr Naggs helped him choose it. And over the years helped him choose many more, and laid them down for him. And when Arthur died, there was quite a cellar of good wine.

Call Me Madam became one of Jack Hylton's great post-war hits, it set a trend that continues today, American entertainment on the West-End stage. It ran for an unprecedented one and a half years, and Arthur had found the actor's Holy Grail: regular employment. Not many actors set their sights for the top, they just pray they won't spend too many months resting.

From Trevor Street they had moved to a slightly bigger flat at Rutland Gate. If you're on Knightsbridge you go up Montpelier Street, turn first left, find a hole-in-the-wall, turn left then right and you're in Rutland Gate. Or you can come down to it from Hyde Park. It sounds frightfully grand and it probably is now, but actors who wanted work had to live in central London, and flats like these could be afforded then.

The only problem with it was that it was up a lot of stairs, past a landing and up more stairs. Joan was pregnant and, shortly after they moved there, I was born.

GREETINGS MRS ARTHUR LOWE QUEEN CHARLOTTES HOSPITAL W6 • CONGRATULATIONS ON EXCELLENT STAGE MANAGEMENT GREETINGS TO STEPHEN AND MUCH LOVE • NEIL •

This meant that she now had to get up all these stairs with David, now eleven years old, me, a push chair and the shopping. But I don't think she would have complained, she'd have just done it. Arthur treated David like his own son, and it was a great joy for Joan to give him another of his very own. Jane could never be forgotten, but it helped.

From the back of the flat you could see right across South London. The people just below us were a Polish couple – we used to pretend he was a spy – he looked like one. He'd invite Arthur and Joan down sometimes in the evenings, and they would sit around and listen to dance-band music on a gramophone. They'd drink orange squash or sometimes sherry. That was the extent of their social life at that time.

There were two rooms, a kitchen and a bathroom all in a long line off a narrow passageway. In the kitchen was a Baby Belling electric cooker and a formica-topped table, my parents' room I can hardly remember, but I know it had a window that opened onto a balcony. On fine days we could sit out on this balcony and watch nannies and children playing in the garden square below. Dad would sit and learn his lines. When he thought he knew them my Mum would take the script from him and he would pace up and down the room with his eyes screwed up while she tested him until he was d.l.p., dead letter perfect.

We all bathed in the early evening before Dad went to the theatre. Then he would set off, a little brown suitcase in his hand. It contained his make-up, just a few simple sticks, an eyebrow pencil and some powder for his shiny pate, an electric egg-boiler in which he brewed his tea, and a novel to read while he was waiting to be called. He was very fond of the W.W. Jacobs *Captain Kettle* stories and Para Handy. He travelled on the tube. Mum would say, 'Break a leg,' and they'd kiss.

No-one ever wishes anybody luck in the theatre, it's thought to work the reverse, just as, 'You were wonderful!' can mean, 'If the audience hadn't been asleep you'd have died.'

Then Mum and I would have our tea and listen to the wireless until it was time for bed. There was an ornate wooden screen, handpainted white by my Mum with gilt decoration, around my bed, and I can remember the security of a familiar eiderdown and blanket. I used to hear my parents' voices late at night.

I have one fearful memory of two ambulance men and a stretcher. Arthur – aware of his responsibilities as the breadwinner – didn't complain of a stomach pain until too late. He was taken away to hospital with a burst appendix. It was 1955, and he was playing in the *Pajama Game* at the Coliseum. It starred Max Wall, Joy Nichols and Edmund Hockridge. Arthur played the Salesman, and they were always singing the numbers at home, 'I'm Not At All In Love', 'Steam Heat', and 'Hernando's Hideaway'. I can hum 'Hernando's Hideaway' now.

Max Wall wrote to him in hospital:

Dear Arthur,
So sorry to hear of your recent operation. These Appendix ops always seem to attack you with no warning, the same happened to my little son aged 6, and he was about an hour away from Peritonitis. Anyhow you are well rid of it although your voice will probably be a lot higher now – *watch that!!*
Here's wishing you well old man – come back soon, your pajamas are being aired.
Salutations!!
Max.

Arthur didn't want his understudy to get too comfortable with the part, and he made some secret arrangements as soon as he could walk to a call-box. We went with Richard Leech, an actor friend since their days at Hereford, in his Lanchester to pick him up from a side door. He was very tough, and totally committed.

In 1954 he'd played Mike in another of these spectacular musicals, *Pal Joey*, produced by Jack Hylton at the Prince's. Most actors would have been content with this level of employment and used the mornings to get in the groceries or walk the dog. Arthur used his mornings to do radio and commercial work. He did BBC Schools broadcasts, various little television jobs and voice-overs for Sharp's Toffee, Summer County and Cadburys – a client he was to keep throughout his working life.

This diversity of work called also for a wide range of technique. Actors needed complete control of their diaphragm and voice, most especially if they were working in radio and television at the same time as performing in un-miked theatres in the evening.

I was talking to David not so long ago, and he said he could remember going onto the stage at the Coliseum when Arthur was playing there and looking out into the vast auditorium. There was no amplification, yet the players had to be able to go out over the top of the orchestra and be heard in every last seat in the house. David also reminded me about the revolve. Oswald Stoll wanted the finest and biggest theatre in London and engaged Frank Matcham to design it. Among its many features it had an amazing three-part revolve, the first of its kind. What a spectacle to see the scene change, complete with chorus line, all folding into each other and then unfolding like the petals of a morning flower as the tables turned in different directions.

1955 and 1956 saw Arthur doing more and more radio and television jobs. More film appearances too: *The Reluctant Bride, Three Women For Joe, One Way Out, Breakaway* and *Who Done It?* In 1956 he didn't appear on the stage at all but had parts in five films: *The High Terrace, The Green Man, Table In The Corner, The Black*

Tide, and *Stranger In Town.* Not to mention a heap of radio and commercial work.

In 1957 he appeared with Paul Scofield in Rodney Ackland's play *A Dead Secret* at the Piccadilly. In a resumé of his career which he wrote himself for the programme of *Bingo* he cites this as the first time he 'really came to notice'.

The plot of the play was built around the Seddons' murder trial, forgotten now except to enthusiasts for crime, and the theme explored the 'Dead Secret', the secret of human personality. Not all the press picked up on Ackland's deeper meaning but it was well received generally, and Paul Scofield's performance earned him good reviews. Philip Hope-Wallace wrote in the (then) Manchester Guardian:

> Rodney Ackland gets a capital play out of a case of suburban poisoning which is bound in outline to recall the Seddon trial. It is about the best thing of its kind – with a magnificent performance by Paul Scofield.

He also singled out 'the mean respectable cousin (beautifully played by Arthur Lowe)'. W.A. Darlington in the Daily Telegraph praised the

> Good work from a large cast: Laidman Browne, Maureen Delaney, Harold Scott, Yvonne Bedford, and Arthur Lowe prominent among them.

Arthur also did quite a bit of sound radio that year but not much television or commercial work. He did no film work at all.

I filled this gap for him by getting a small part myself in *A Night To Remember*, the film about the sinking of the Titanic with Kenneth More in the lead. Honor Blackman played my Mum, and I had two gorgeous sisters with cherries in their hats and I was in love with both of them. I am indecently proud of the fact that I fell in love so young, and so plurally. A chauffeur-driven car used to collect me and my Mum, who was paid as a chaperone. Sometimes it was an Austin Siddeley, but sometimes it was a Rolls-Royce. It took us to the lot at Pinewood after dark. The scenes on the tilting deck were shot in the evening in winter so everybody's breath would steam.

It must have been now that we moved to Pavilion Road. It's all changed now of course, but if you walk north along Sloane Street and take a turning off left towards Harrods you find yourself crossing a long, narrow street which runs parallel with Sloane Street. Above a carpet store, in through a narrow door and up a flight of stone stairs, a small landing opened out onto a roof garden. Another door from this same landing opened into a large room which was to become our dining room and kitchen. From this a staircase led up to another big room with high windows of French pro-portions. After traversing this room you came to a slype, which took you through to another passageway and another huge room. There was a tiny lavatory at one end of this passageway and a stairway at the other. By descending this stair you came to a dank self-contained flat of two rooms, and a bathroom and kitchen, the door of which opened out onto the roof garden you en-countered when first you mounted the stone stair from the street.

It was derelict and strange and entirely to my parents' liking. By virtue of the fact that it had been a brothel and that one of the poor girls had jumped to her death in the street below, it had remained empty for some time and the lease was offered on very reasonable terms. Most significant of all, the telephone exchange was Belgravia, so the prefix BEL sent an immediate message to managements, and who knows – it may even have improved their offers.

It became Arthur's First Great Project. He acquired a clipboard and got the telephone reconnected at once. Builders, plumbers, electricians and all trades to Tooting descended on the place. Joan, drawing on her experience in wartime stage-management, where everything had to be begged, borrowed, stolen or improvised, devised extraordinary furnishings for the place which could never be forgotten by anyone who ever saw them. Dreary wooden pillars would be covered with marble-effect Contact and flutings painted in at their base, and from six feet away the result was convincing. Sheeshee lampshades were stripped of their fabric, and the frames were woven with coarse string. It made a lovely, rambling home for two boys – David was at home quite often at that time, home from grammar school in Hexham, when he lived with his Gran, and later when he was down from Balliol – and with no neighbours it was a place where my Mum could breathe, and play the piano and sing, and David could practise at the piano at all hours, and I could have my railway set up properly on a big table bought from Tulley's for thirty bob.

The big room off the top passageway had been made into two bedrooms by erecting a partition, and from my window I overlooked the street. In the early mornings

I could lean out and see the ice arrive at Searcy, the posh caterers, on a horse-drawn cart and watch for the milkman coming along. Both drivers knew me and would call up cheerily, whistling as they went about their business. Their horses' shoes rang on the cobbles and echoed off Harrod's depository, no longer there. In the wet the horses sometimes slipped, and their shoes made another noise again.

The little lavatory on the top landing had been done out by Joan like a Chinese Temple. Arthur, scrabbling about on a demolition site around the corner, had come home with a strange iron thing with coloured glass set in it. He had soon converted it into a very satisfactory lampshade for the light in this unusual loo. Because the house had previously been of ill-repute we already had trouble with the doorbell being rung late at night by callers who had not caught up with the news of its new occupancy. Now the problem was increased by the shadowy red light in an upstairs window, the light cast by the weird lampshade in the Chinese loo. One night Arthur, fed up with these disturbances, went down and, with Anglo-Saxon economy, told the man to go away without delay.

'Don't you speak to me like that,' the man shouted. 'If you were a younger a man I'd take you out into the street'.

'Alright then, out into the street it is,' Arthur shouted back. Leaning out of my window I could just make out the main players in this little altercation. The smaller man suddenly took a sidestep and gave a quick left and a right, which sounded as if they both connected. The other figure made off down the street, the front door slammed, and Arthur, his territory defended, came up the stairs to bed. At breakfast the next morning he had plasters over his knuckles, but he was puffed up with pride and Mum was unusually attentive. They were like two pigeons.

Across the road at the Forge Café the people bought one of the new television sets – it was now the late fifties – and as a special treat we would go over in the early evening to watch Arthur in *The Diamond Bird* or *All Aboard*. In *All Aboard* he played Sydney Barker the steward on a passenger ship, the SS Adriana. He used to go off to do these sequences aboard the 'Rangitoto' of the New Zealand Shipping Company when she was lying at KG5. King George V Docks came to mean a lot to us: Ellerman City Line had company sheds there and Dad would come to see me when my ship was berthed. Looking back through the cast list other names catch the eye: Gordon Jackson, Susannah York, and Terence Alexander. Richard O'Sullivan, with whom Arthur was later to play in *Doctor At Large,* appeared as a passenger. In the days of steam-TV all the location stuff was filmed in advance, and then the programme went out live with the pre-filmed bits inserted as appropriate, so I grew up happily accepting the idea that my Dad had gone to work at the studios, and here was I at the neighbours', watching him on a tiny green-tinted screen contained in an enormous veneer cabinet. Although techniques were crude by the standards we apply today, the performances were more vibrant because of the adrenaline brought on by playing live to an audience of a million or more.

My mother continued in her belief that television was a pernicious device, a poor corruption of the cinema and a prostitution of the actor's art. Reluctant to waste her money – as telly-visions were obviously going to be discontinued at any moment – it was sometime before we acquired a set of our own. Even when we did it was hidden away behind curtains. A weakness, of which we should be thoroughly ashamed.

Television was to become the mainstay of Arthur's work. His subtle delivery and tricksy facial expressions were ideally suited to the new close-shot medium. He enjoyed the workplace of the studio floor, and he liked the factory feel of the television centres with their canteens and egalitarian style.

For a while our lives seemed charmed. This big bohemian flat, the roof garden so hot in summer that sweetcorn and tomatoes grew in tubs, Arthur in work, David at Oxford, me at a good school in Sussex, a happy circle of friends for parties and the bistro. On Saturday afternoons we met the Shines in the park and played cricket, on Sunday mornings we went to the pub before lunch.

Arthur was showing the first but happy signs of being a foodie. Not five minutes walk from our door were Harrods Food Halls; and the splendiferous displays in the Fishmongers' Hall and the smell of the ground coffee and the colourful arrays of confectionery were a greater temptation than he could bear. The men at the counters came to know and like him. He enjoyed marketeers of every sort, a liking inherited from his father, and the exchanges that accompanied each transaction would have made the script for a sitcom in themselves.

'Tell me, how much is the salmon a pound?'

'Five shillings, Mr Lowe.'

'Five shillings?' Taking a step back in amazement.

'Come all the way from Scotland, ennit?'

63

'Well it must have travelled first class.'

'Alright then, Mr Lowe, four and six to you.'

He would bring home a brace of pheasants and a grouse to make the gravy, smoked salmon which had been sliced as he watched with the long serrated blades he so admired, and a quarter of sugared almonds for my mother.

'Those cost nearly a pound a pound, you know,' he would tell her proudly.

Joanie would say, 'When we were children in Rhyl we used to get edible pebbles. I think we used to pay tuppence ha'penny a quarter.'

But Arthur's work was to become the tail that wagged the dog, and these halcyon days were just the calm before the storm. He was taking more and more television work, and one major change had taken place: Arthur now had an agent.

He was in preparation at the Arts Theatre for the Henry Livings play, *Stop It Whoever You Are*. Henry recalls Arthur's new agent creeping into the stalls and then trying to persuade the producer, Michael Codron, to hold off his decision on the casting for his play until the end of the week because he wanted Arthur released to begin on a new television series in the North of England.

'Tell your client,' said Michael Codron to the creep, 'I strongly recommend that he takes this.'

They had been quite stunned by Arthur's performance, which had been tailored for him by Livings, and they didn't want to lose him now. One critic was to say, when he saw the show on its first night, that he didn't believe Mr Lowe was an actor at all. He was a Manchester Alderman who had missed his way at Euston and strayed by accident onto the stage at the Arts Theatre. As it turned out it was to be one of Arthur's major stage performances and a significant – if not disastrous – turning point in his life and career. The agent, Jimmy Lavall, could see only the money.

Granada offered Arthur the part – quite a minor part at that time – of the draper and lay preacher Leonard Swindley, in *Coronation Street*.

I can remember heated arguments at home. For a start, it would mean Arthur working for much of the time in Manchester. Would Joan go too? Would they leave London and this lovely flat and move north? Jimmy Lavall argued in favour of the part in *Coronation Street*. Anybody with a business head could see which would be the more lucrative; stage work or television. Joan's argument – that Arthur's unique talent would be wasted in a 'soap-opera' – lost some of its force because everybody knew she didn't want to be left alone, nor to move to Manchester.

'She loved me for the dangers I had pass'd. And I loved her that she did pity them.'

Joan loved Arthur because she recognised in him his dizzying talent as a straight actor. He loved her that she knew that. She didn't want to see this dissipated on some serial studio floor. If she could have looked further ahead and seen how this would lead to *Turn Out The Lights, Potter* and *Bless Me Father*, not to mention advertising Lyons' Pie Mix and Clearasil, she would certainly have fought to the death to stop that move. If she had won the day and Arthur had stayed playing the London stage, his would have been a greater discipline, he would have been fitter, mentally and physically.

But how can I be so selfish? He would have given pleasure only to thousands – and they the literati – not to the millions that sat farting into their sofas with the effort of laughing. I am sorry, television viewers, if I offend you – I rant at myself too – but there is nothing quite so gut-wrenching as wasted opportunity.

Our lives now changed. He had been known as Mr Lowe until this time, or Arthur to his friends. People in the street had behaved as they do with the rest of us, maybe catching our eye and exchanging some small greeting, or averting their gaze, or just going about their busy day. Now they stared. Their heads panned round, gurning at him, and then they tripped over the kerb. They pointed. They smirked. They invariably got it wrong.

'Would you sign this for my little girl?' (or their aunty, or their mother, never for themselves), 'I do enjoy your music.'

'My music?'

'Here, someone said you were Leonard Swingle'.

We had taken to riding in the Rotten Row, but now when we rode our horses out around Hyde Park Corner the cabbies leant out of their cabs, one arm on the window.

'Blow me! It's Mr Swindley on a 'orse!'

It was the end of our private lives together.

4

'*I planned a long return to the theatre*'

1958–1967

IN 1958 Arthur had been working on the picture, *The Boy And The Bridge,* with his friend Bill Shine. Their costumes were the blue overalls and caps of the bridge-keepers, and they were very comfortable in their roles. It was summer, and like Ratty they thought what a grand life it was by the river. Leaning on the teak rails of Tower Bridge they could watch the cranes working the Ellerman Pappayani ships as they lay at the wharves, the needs of a city being discharged and the fruit of its labours waiting on the quay for export. Brown, tattooed sailors moved about the decks applying grease and paint, and their officers also leant on the rails and surveyed the passing tugs and lighters.

It stirred the sleeping sailor in Arthur, and in the evenings he would spread brochures out on the table in the dining room and plan sea-voyages. It has all but slipped away now, but in those balmy salt-sea days when Britain was a maritime nation with a merchant navy, it was possible for not more than twelve passengers to embark on certain cargo ships and, if not in luxury then in reasonable comfort, visit the various foreign ports that were the ship's regular trade. Joan too loved the sea, and together they planned these voyages late into the night. It was 1961 before we embarked on the first of these trips, in the 'Freesia' to Copenhagen, Aarhus and Odense.

The North Sea was calm and foggy and I, aged eight, snivelled all the way, comforted by my mother as the blast of the fog horn ripped through my shivering frame. Dad wore his habitual flat suede cap and jacket and let the sea air empty his overloaded head and refill it with a spirit of adventure. A man's man, he befriended Larson the bosun, and the two made a heart-warming sight for a frightened boy as they sat on the hatchboards and chattered away in pigeon English, my short father animated beside this gentle toothless giant. I was taken to my cabin early because in the saloon the jokes were getting blue, and the drink aboard a Danish ship is not allowed to rot in the bottles. When we docked at Copenhagen and went ashore it was very dull and very expensive, but we were all thrilled, so great was our adventure.

I don't know just how the dates of this voyage fit in with *Stop It Whoever You Are* at the Arts and those first episodes of *Coronation Street* – does it really matter? It was a crossroads in our lives, and it all melds into one moment in history for me.

Michael Codron and Henry Livings hadn't heard of *Coronation Street* until Jimmy Lavall had spoken of it. They probably weren't that interested.

Up in Manchester – operating on a different plane altogether – a man called Tony Warren had re-jigged an earlier script called *Our Street*, which had been rejected by the BBC. He'd gone with producer Harry Elton to Granada with the idea and, armed with a one paragraph synopsis (they say the best ideas can be written on the back of a fag packet) it had gone ahead on a trial basis. All that was needed was to find the right name for the street itself:

'A fascinating freemasonry, a volume of unwritten rules. These are the driving forces behind the life in a working-class street in the north of England. The purpose of "Florizel Street" is to examine a community of this nature, and to entertain.'

And to use – I think for the first time – regional actors operating in standard mode. Granada had a commitment, a worthy commitment, to reflect the life of the area it served. Britain was entering a new dark age – from which it is yet to emerge – when television entertainment would no longer be uplifting or enlightening. Just a self-gratifying, narcissistic replay of our daily lives.

I hope we're all going to remember Arthur C. Clarke in our prayers. Thank you God for Arthur C. Clarke and for bestowing upon him the vision to invent the communications satellite. And thank you for the rocket men and women who have dedicated their lives to sticking them up there in geo-whatsit orbit.

Because if we'd had to rely on the terrestrial channels we'd all be watching *Neighbours, Brookside, EastEnders, Home And Away, Coronation Street* ad infinitum. The banality of it all could split your head.

Perhaps, when all the country is cabled, we will have a bigger choice again. Then the programmers may find enough bandwidth for the arts.

A framed pencil drawing of a street – *The Street* – hung

on our wall at home. It's quite pleasing, with the Mission of Glad Tidings in the left foreground and the chilling South Face of a cotton mill accelerating away to a disappearing point at the end of a row of terraced houses. On the opposite side of the street is a shop with enamel signs advertising the standard appeasements: Players cigarettes and Guinness. This is the opposite end to The Rover's Return. In this picture you have everything: habitation, toil, religion and weakness of the flesh.

It was into this world that Leonard Swindley was born. Of parents Thomas and Eliza-Jane Swindley of 16, Clark Street, Weatherfield on 9 December 1916. One year three months younger than the actor who played him. Who came from just around around the corner, a local boy. Who pushed a handcart for a cotton mill in the depression years. Politically correct.

To me Arthur was an actor. He went to the theatre or the studios. Put on his make-up and his costume. Portrayed someone else for an hour or two. Took it all off again and got in a taxi and came home.

The question I am most asked is:

'Was he like that in real life?'

If I think the inquisitor is man enough to take it, I reply, 'Fuck off!'

Arthur appeared in around ninety episodes of *Coronation Street*. He gave it the commitment he gave everything he played and so, with time, the writers, Tony Warren and Harry Kershaw, built the part up. He became an unforgettable part of a serial that has run for thirty-five years now, since first it went out at 7 p.m. on Friday 9 December 1960 – Leonard Swindley's 44th birthday.

The theme tune can be recalled and whistled by almost every person in the land. Fifteen writers and three story-liners work on it, there's a full-time archivist. You can go on a tour of the set; Hollywood, California has come to Deansgate, Manchester. The show is seen all over the world. When my wife first came to England from New Zealand the first thing she recognised were the rooftops with their chimney stacks: just like *Coronation Street*.

As a family it set us up financially, and I don't recall us ever again being short of money.

But the separation was doing Joan no good. I found a letter Arthur had written. I'm reluctant to share it with you, but I want to show you how much they were in love because it's going to be important later. It's in Arthur's neat handwriting, and he's crossed some things out and replaced them. The replacements change the whole meaning. It shows how cruel changes in his schedule could be:

> The Prescription (to be taken when feeling low).
> Darling Pony,
> I really do understand how much you hate to be alone and I'm terribly sorry not to show it more. It's a rotten trick of fate to have arranged my work this way and I would give anything for it not to be so. Please try not to fret too much – today will soon be over, then ~~I'll~~ you will be ~~home on Friday~~ with the children. We've had a much happier time these last few days – let's ~~have a~~ go on being happy! ~~weekend?~~
> I love you very dearly   Tim
>   xxxxxxxxxxx
> P.S. I think you handled the press magnificently
>   xxx

He had signed it 'Tim', which he did when he was at his most tender.

Henry Livings witnessed one of these cruel moments. Arthur, after a foul day working with a director with a twitch, had left without waiting for a wrap. I suppose this is unforgivable, to just walk off the set, an anarchic vein that occasionally surfaced. He'd been having a wash in his cabin on the sleeper – was going to have a sherry and some supper after the train pulled out – when he was taken off by two coppers, back to the set to do yet another take of a scene that just wouldn't go right.

> Arthur came up to Henry where he stood, in the open area where the cameras manoeuvred from setting to setting. 'All right then, Henry, just a quick chorus, "Abide With Me", I'll take the cornet, you're on trombone.' He jiggled his imaginary keys to be sure the valves were free, cocked a solemn eye to see if Henry's slide was mobile and ready to play, opened and blew through his imaginary spit-valve, with a grave *moue* of apology for the pool of imaginary spit at Henry's feet, pressed his imaginary instrument to his lips, blew out his cheeks like Dizzy Gillespie, nodded, and they were off. Arthur's wavering, mournful, un-warmed-up cornet soared in B flat among the cobwebs, Henry's extended fart of the harmony labouring up after it.
> *Henry Livings, 'The Rough Side of the Boards'*

We all moved up to Manchester but kept the place in Pavilion Road on. Arthur's motto: if in doubt, do both. We rented a suburban house on the Wilmslow Road. It was quite alien to me, I'd lived only in flats done up by my mother, and the crushingly dull decor of the place affected us all very badly. There was a bar in the lounge – we'd never had a lounge before, only living rooms – and the bath was Como Blue instead of white, which is the only colour for a bath. In desperation Joan threw herself at the garden, but we even had a gardener. She and Arthur had some stinking rows in that house. I was glad when we left.

Arthur didn't mix much. He filled the car, the house, her life with flowers. Anywhere Joanie went flowers followed her, but she lived only for the six months out.

> 'Well, with Swindley in *Coronation Street* I had a contract with Granada, which meant I only had to do it for six months in every year, so unlike the rest of that cast I could get back to the theatre for at least half of my time. When first they offered it to me I thought *Coronation Street* was going to be a local show for Manchester only: then after the success of the first few years they peeled Swindley off into his own series, and I did that for a while. But managements in the theatre have been very good to me; they all knew me before the TV series so they think of me as a character actor, not as a tele-star who can't do anything else.'
>
> *Interview with Sheridan Morley*

The Swindley spin-off was *Pardon The Expression* with Betty Driver, Joy Stewart and Paul Dawkins. Now he was assistant manager of Dobson and Hawks, the writers could build on Swindley's self-importance. He had some cracking writers too, Harry Driver, Jack Rosenthal and Christopher Bond. But from the first read-through Arthur started cutting any funny lines that were not his own, especially Betty's. She says he had aide-mémoires hidden around the set and was generally pretty awkward to work with. Bob Dorning came and played Paul's part in the next series, the character of Ernest Parbold was translated into Walter Hunt. It ran for thirty-two episodes. Betty says Arthur never bought her a cup of tea the whole time it ran. But then he wasn't a cup of tea man; he used his spare moments to ring his agent.

Arthur and Bob then went on to do *Turn Out The Lights*. An expression of my grandfather's which my Dad adopted was, 'It's only one orange, and when you've squeezed it, the juice is gone.' Sacked from Dobson and Hawks, Hunt and Swindley became ghost-hunters, the juice was indeed gone. Swindley died an ignominious death.

Arthur told a newspaper reporter,

> 'I didn't want to do any more Swindley. I thought it would take a long time before the image of Swindley had worn off. I planned a long return to the theatre.'

The six-months-on, six-months-off contract was fiendishly clever because not only did it allow for re-negotiation of the fee twice a year, it had acted as an evil-eye to the spirit world of the type-cast, the walking dead of the soaps. Arthur emerged virtually unscathed – professionally speaking, at least.

A number of happy accidents occurred during the *Coronation Street* and *Pardon the Expression* years. One of them was the disappearance of Jimmy Lavall, though it had to be paid for in hard currency.

Dodo Watts – who was head of casting at ABC – put a young man called Peter Campbell in touch with Jimmy, who was needing an assistant. Peter thought the post held promise because Lavall had some talent on his books: Hugh Manning, Hermione Baddeley, and Arthur Lowe. He also had a drink problem. After lunch you had to forget him or hide him.

Peter was a bit surprised – but moved with the caution one does when in a new job – to find he wasn't allowed near the books. Jimmy had an alcoholic bank manager and an alcoholic accountant, and the three of them used to go off and form a coven together. Peter had started in the May, and just before Christmas some money had come in. The cheques were made out for the artists and were sitting there waiting for Jimmy to sign. Peter took a couple of days off over Christmas, and when he went into the office just before New Year there were the cheques still sitting on the desk – unsigned. While Peter sat there, wondering what he might best do, Jimmy rang from a pub across the road.

'Bring two sheets of paper and two sixpenny stamps,' he said.

Peter collected the paper and the stamps and went into the pub. Jimmy had already had quite a few drinks.

'Fucking actors,' he said. 'I've had enough of them.'

He wrote one letter signing the business over to Peter and signed across the stamp. He wrote the other to his accountant. He reached into his jacket pocket and showed Peter a bottle of pills.

'I'm going to catch a plane to Johannesburg,' this was where he came from. 'If you try to stop me I'll take these.'

Later Peter met one of Jimmy's friends. He had caught the plane, he said.

Peter covered for him for a few days but with no money in the account to pay the artists he called in Equity. Jimmy rang from South Africa – reversing the charge – to wish him a Happy New Year. Then after a while, worse than being gone, he was back. Peter got a call to say he was staying in rooms at Paddington. Shortly after, Jimmy was admitted to a home for the incurable.

Peter thinks it was about £2000 of Arthur's money that Jimmy ran off with (Arthur was owed the most). Henry Livings thinks it was £600. Either way, that was a lot in the 1960's. Arthur helped Peter get set up, and Peter remained Arthur's agent and friend right up to Arthur's death in 1982.

Another happy accident was meeting the actor, director and film-maker, Lindsay Anderson.

Lindsay had seen Arthur's Alderman Oglethorpe in *Stop It Whoever You Are* at the Arts,

> . . . He played an incredibly pompous north countryman quite superbly – it was really acting, it wasn't just a caricature at all . . .
>
> *Lindsay Anderson in an interview*
> *with Bill Pertwee*

Lindsay was casting for David Storey's *This Sporting Life*, and he offered Arthur the part of Slomer in what was to be a film about what Leslie Halliwell calls an 'unattractive hero in a grim setting' .

> I realised at once that this was something much more complex, and much more distinguished than the story of a footballer's success and

disillusion which the advance note had suggested . . . The central character, Frank Machin, was immensely striking, with an ambiguity of nature, half overbearing, half acutely sensitive, that fascinated me, without my being fully aware that I understood him. The same was true of his tortured, impossible relationship with the woman in the story; a bleak, Northern affair, of powerful, inarticulate emotions frustrated or deformed by puritanism and inhibition. The background rough and hard: no room here for charm or sentimental proletarianism. It was an intimidating subject for a film. I was not sure I would be up to it.

> *Lindsay Anderson in 'The Films Of Lindsay Anderson' by Elizabeth Sussex (Studio Vista)*

I have trouble watching the film through because so skilful was Lindsay that the suppressed violence – 'the motif of force' – grates the bone. Richard Harris played the lead part of Frank Machin and Arthur, true to style, made the most of a small but crucial part:

> The board of directors of the rugby league club were all local businessmen, with Weaver as director and by far the most forceful of them. It was his support that got Machin on the team. The only director ever to oppose Weaver's decisions was the gruff Slomer, and he took against Machin and what he stood for from the first. Their disagreement in this matter kept surfacing through the film.
>
> *Jeremy Perkins, 'Internet Movie Database'*

In the end though it is only Slomer who keeps him in the team. It is totally different from any other British film of the period. The editing is complex and audiences were ready to accept Lindsay's techniques which went way beyond straight story telling.

> *This Sporting Life* is the most passionate film ever to have emerged from a British studio, and all Anderson's previous experience in the theatre and cinema must have come into play to make it such a very remarkable feature film debut.
>
> *'The Films Of Lindsay Anderson'*

On the 13 April 1963 Lindsay wrote this letter to Arthur, c/o *Coronation Street*:

> Very nice to hear from you (even if I do have to reply to Coronation Street!)
> Naturally the announcements about *Wuthering Heights* are premature, but have no doubt that when the time comes for casting you will be prominent in my mind. I don't know if you have managed to see *This Sporting Life* yet, but you certainly made an enormous and much appreciated contribution to it.
> I am delighted to hear you will be at the Court for the Livings play, and look forward to seeing you then.

Arthur never rested; it seems he had seized at a mention of Lindsay's plans to film *Wuthering Heights* to put himself in the mind's eye for casting. As it happens it was never made. The Livings play referred to by Lindsay was *Kelly's Eye* which opened at the Royal Court on 12 June 1963.

Arthur played – 'with alarming accuracy' – a blind Scotsman, the narrator; Nicol Williamson justly received rave reviews; Sarah Miles convinced most but not all; the theatre was full every night.

Here was Arthur at his best, walking the half mile from 35, Pavilion Road to the Royal Court in Sloane Square and back again after the show, doing what he loved and knew best, playing the theatre. The same year he played beside Nicol Williamson again at the Royal Court in *Inadmissible Evidence,* John Osborne's fourth full-length play, following *Look Back In Anger, The Entertainer,* and *Luther.*

Arthur played two parts, the Judge at the opening of the play and Hudson, chief clerk in the solicitor's office, presided over by Williamson, and gave something special to each, receiving recognition from everyone who saw it. Anthony Page, who directed the show, wrote to him:

> As you know, I cannot imagine anyone playing Hudson after the marvellous way you created it, and I hope tremendously you will be able to come America with it, as I am sure you would have an immense success. And of course, I shall let you know any news about the film, as soon as it begins to be crystalized.
>
> Please give my love to Joan. Thank you again for the marvellous performances you gave at the Court, which are some of the best I have ever had anything to do with.

In a career decision which it is not for me to judge, but which in cold shrinking moments I fear may have been made because of my school fees, Arthur decided to go back to *Coronation Street* and not to go to America with *Inadmissible Evidence*. John Osborne wrote him a desperately sad letter:

> My dear Arthur,
> Thank you v. much indeed for your note. I have been so horrified that things should have come to this pass, sp. [specially] after all the efforts that were made to avoid it months ago. It seems awful, and I can only say it seems very glum indeed to think of the play without you. You brought such authority and sensibility with you that is so rare I mustn't go on. What a wicked thing we are all in. However dear Arthur, thank you with all my heart. It *will* never be the same, but there. I do hope the series goes well and enjoyably (I'm starting watching *The Street* now). Perhaps we may do something again one day. We've just moved in to the new house. You must come round when you can. [Illegible] . . . Love to Joan.
>
> Affectionately, John.

Lindsay Anderson, by now a real devotee of the Arthur Lowe method of acting, recalled the performance in an interview with Bill Pertwee for his *Life Of Arthur Lowe* on radio:

> I remember in the first production of *Inadmissible Evidence* with Nicol Williamson – Arthur

played his elder partner and also the judge in the prologue of the play and he gave it a . . . a bite and an acidity . . . an edge which I shouldn't think it has ever had again. I'll always remember when Nicol Williamson hesitated at the beginning and the Judge came in with the single word – which I couldn't possibly imitate I'm afraid – but the word was 'mediocrity'. And this spoken by Arthur had an impact and a cutting edge that I don't think anyone else could do. If Arthur had a good part nobody would be better. He was really one of our finest actors.

*

At this hour of the morning there is no-one on the cobbled streets of Le Havre. Ahead of me are the tail lights – bright red reflecting off the wet setts – of other trucks heading South. I wonder what journeys their drivers are making.

I'm tempted to run along beside the Seine but I've got too far to go, I should try to be somewhere like Auxerre tonight or beyond and into Italy tomorrow. Before I left the overnight ferry I filled my flask, and now that I'm coming out of the docks and onto the smooth metal of the main road I can pour hot black coffee into the cup that sits in a special holder on the gearbox casing to my right. Winding down the window I can light a cigarette and blow the smoke out into the cold air of the hour before dawn.

There are conflicting reports and I can't see why. Henry says he was as sharp as a knife, Lindsay says

'Arthur's Edge', but Betty says he had to read his lines off the desk. I didn't know that this business of not being able to learn his lines went so far back. Henry's a spade's-a-spade man, and Arthur was his idol. Lindsay had declared Dad one of our finest actors. Maybe Betty's got a little axe to grind? No, not so she'd invent that. Anyway I've heard it before, and since. I've seen it for myself, a masterful pause narrowly swerving away from a dry.

A horrid little car with a cold engine pulls out right in front of me and stalls. In a split second which takes a lifetime to unfold I know I cannot, dare not – thirty tons up on a wet road – brake that hard. In my mirror there's another truck alongside my trailer, and as my eyes go back to witness the inevitable I get the headlight flash I need from the truck behind and pull left and miss the car. I blink a thank you to the driver behind and pull back into the right to let him past. The 'him' is a 'her', the lady driver from last night, blonde curls and a wicked grin. She makes a gesture which says it all. Knights and knightesses of the road, she with more power, me with more time.

I reach for my flask and cigarettes and congratulate myself and my colleague on our quick reactions. Adrenaline, maybe that's the difference. Maybe theatre makes the happy hormone flow, Lindsay's intensity and the smell of celluloid. Maybe a long, dull day in a television studio fails to feed the rat.

It's a long road that lies ahead, and it's paved with misconceptions. What was he like, why was he how he was? Well, he changed, and his aspirations grew. He wasn't fixed in time and space, and I'd failed to see that at first.

*

Each New Year's Day my parents held a cracking drinks party for all their friends. The big upstairs room made the perfect place for it. The Black Velvet and the conversation flowed.

These were stand-around parties, done for their old friends. Where the kids push through a sea of legs, cigarette smoke and intense chattering, bearing nuts and olives, the new generation meeting the old, collecting their tribal stuff. A nine-year-old blonde in silk taffeta – the spit image of her mother – saying to an olive-skinned boy with tight black curls,

'Darling, I felt so persecuted.'

A deep, fatherly voice, from a few people away,

'Jennifer if you have any more champagne I think it will be a big mistake. Will you please change to orange juice.'

Toke Townley, a dear actor they had met in their early days in rep. Trotter Rutter, a friend of Joanie's, who'd left the theatre to be a tour guide with a big American firm. The Shines: Bill had worked with Arthur on *The Boy And The Bridge*, he'd written a show called *Ireland, Your Name Is Magic* and wanted my brother David to work on the score. Terry and June Alexander. Bob and Honor Dorning and their daughters: Stacy Dorning had an acting career, you may remember her as William's sister Ethel in *Just William* and there is a sampler 'To Arthur and Joan Lowe' done by Kate Dorning hanging in their cabin aboard the 'Amazon' now. Only a few personal treasures, and nothing of the theatre, in this, their last bastion of privacy. Christopher Bond, and his son Trevor, later to become a film editor and to work with Arthur on the *Mister Men* films. Richard and Helen Leech (Helen Uttley), whom they first met at Hereford, and their daughters. Richard, a lovely actor who gave a rounded, big performance, amongst other things as Mr Rochester in the TV serialisation of *Jane Eyre*, shared with Arthur an interest in cine film-making, and taught him many of the basic skills of editing and synchronising the sound. Ritchie Gatehouse, Joan's first husband, and his new wife Barbara Bliss, daughter of Sir Arthur Bliss. Colin Douglas, his wife and numerous offspring. Marguerite Stone, another old chum from Hereford. Lindsay Anderson. Peter Campbell and Felicity, his assistant in the office. My godfather Neil Wilson and his wife Molly. I wish I could remember every one of the people who were there.

In that interview with Bill Pertwee, Lindsay said,

> After *This Sporting Life* I really knew that I never wanted to do anything – I never wanted to make a film – without Arthur in it.

Salford made a strange sight when the bulldozers moved in, all the houses were gone but on every street corner a pub still stood, protected by its licence. This was the setting for Lindsay Anderson's next film, the *The White Bus*. It was part of a trilogy proposed by Oscar Lewenstein and originally meant for each of the 'Free Cinema' directors, Lindsay being one of them. 'Free Cinema' was a title Lindsay coined when he was a contributor to Sequence magazine; the first Free Cinema programme was shown at the National Film Theatre in 1956, the same year that John Osborne's *Look Back In Anger* was put on at the Royal Court. By choosing the word 'free' Lindsay was trying to put across an idea of 'personal', free from the constraints on style imposed by the major studios and distributors. Shelagh Delaney's story of a girl returning to her home town and joining a conducted bus tour fell to Lindsay, and he started work with Delaney who wrote her own screenplay. It's a complex film, switching between fantasy and reality, between black and white and colour, and it never got proper distribution.

> There is a public for *The White Bus,* but not a
> public that, say, United Artists are in any way in
> touch with . . . It is the kind of film I wanted to
> make and am quite proud of having made . . .
> the kind of work that in telling a story has
> bigger implications. *Lindsay Anderson*

Though the fees were not in line with the spoils of television, it was also the sort of film Arthur wanted to be in – there was still hope for a British Cinema driven by the New Left then – he saw it as a career path that he wanted to follow. Arthur was terribly good as the mayor in *The White Bus,* in a role that came to him easily, and he enjoyed working in his boyhood surround. He also liked Lindsay very much. They shared certain things: patriotism, total commitment, a streak of anarchy – and a need to do television commercials to eat between more interesting assignments. Both men saw these commercials as a genre in their own right and gave as much to these jobs as they gave to the arts.

The young Czech cameraman Miroslav Ondricek shot *The White Bus* and also Lindsay's next British-made film *If . . . .* They had formed a close bond. Lindsay hated having to explain things to people to the extent that he just didn't do it, and with Ondricek he enjoyed sublime communication. With his actors he directed, but always in a collaborative way, and this may be one reason he enjoyed Arthur so much, because Arthur needed no direction in the conventional sense. Indeed he thought that the best use for most directors was to guard his copy of the script until morning.

If . . . was made, as it happens, partly at the school I was presently attending. Arthur played the ineffectual housemaster, Mr Kemp, who allows his sadistic prefects to gain power. The scene that stays with me is of Mr Kemp sitting up in bed with Mrs Kemp, played by Mary MacLeod, and blowing the recorder. He had a devil of a job to learn the thing and sat up in bed, just as in the film, with my mother beside him beating out the time. The part demonstrated his tremendous versatility. He had become associated with pompous characters, even in Lindsay's mind when he cast him as the mayor in *The White Bus*. But here he was equally as good, better, playing a weak character who distinctly lacked pomp. David Wood – who played one of the central trio of rebels, the boys who receive the most dreadful thrashing at the hands of the head boy, not for any offence, but for their bad attitude – wrote to me:

> I was thrilled when I found out I was going to work with him. I well remember a scene that took place in the school hall/dining hall. All the pupils were there, including the professional actors as well as extras – schoolboys from the school we were filming in, Aldenham, near Watford.
>
> The school staff were also present. Your father played the House Master, who was quite

Arthur Lowe at home, 1916   At Hayfield, c.1935

With Daisy, the pony that never saw action

The desert life

A very sharp mind

The Mercury Theatre, Alexandria

The ideal character actor, short and bald

Joan Cooper

Stephen, *A Night to Remember*

The roof garden, 33-35 Pavilion Road

Dr. Munda,
O Lucky Man

Hudson,
Inadmissible Evidence

Leonard Swindley, *Coronation Street*

Capt. Mainwaring, relaxing with the irascible crowd

Dogberry, *Much Ado About Nothing*

clearly a mild-mannered man, dominated by the strict disciplinarianism of Rowntree, the Head Prefect. He made a rather nervous speech of welcome to everybody, particularly the new boys.

Your father's performance, from the very first rehearsal, was so funny, not in an overt way, but in its reality and sincerity. I remember that Malcolm McDowell, Richard Warwick and I were all standing listening by a table near the front. We started corpsing, unable to contain our laughter at your father's performance. It really was splendidly funny.

Lindsay Anderson became very annoyed with us for interrupting the scene, and after several repeat performances of uncontrollable giggling, we were kicked out of the hall and threatened with loss of our reaction close-ups!

What stuck in David's mind though, so that it still bothered him, was something that had happened during a break from shooting . . .

Because we were filming in a school – Alden-ham, as I said earlier – we had no dressing rooms and no green room in which to relax when we were not actually filming. The pro-duction company were not lavishing money on the production, so that we had no caravans on location either. The only place we could all go for a sit, a chat and a rest, was the school library. I well remember your father, who did not mix with us 'boys', sitting on his own at

87

one end of the library, thinking through his lines or simply keeping calm. Meanwhile we, at the other end, were part of a group of young actors. I expect we spoke rather loudly, having little consideration for the feelings of the older members of the cast.

We started criticising Aldenham. We had been filming in a dormitory, which had looked so ghastly, with peeling green (I think) paint, that Lindsay Anderson had asked for it to be completely repainted, because he didn't want the audience to think that he was exaggerating when painting his picture of a spartan minor public school. We had also filmed the shower scene in the rather unpleasant semi-outdoor showers, which we all felt were unsuitable in a so-called civilized society!

The conversation ended up with us all agreeing that none of us would ever dream of sending our own children to Aldenham, that any parent who did so would show no humane feelings whatsoever!

Only later did someone tell him that Arthur had a son at the school and he realised that Arthur must have overheard everything that was said! I was able to confirm that this had, indeed, been the case. Dad never mentioned it.

The moneybags behind *If* . . . was Memorial Enterprises, comprising Albert Finney and Michael Medwin, but distribution was sticky. CBS came forward at one point but then suddenly pulled out – after they read the script, it's said – and eventually Paramount took it on.

The budget was just £250,000 and to save on the cost of repainting a lot of the locations (it was shot at three different schools) it was shot partly in black and white. If it hadn't been for management's eye to future markets, Lindsay – who was not a good judge of colour anyway – would have been perfectly happy to shoot the whole film in black and white. That's a kick in the backside for the analysts who constructed subtle theories that the shifts between colour and monochrome indicated the distinction between reality and fantasy. Lindsay simply said of the film: 'It's all real.'

It was 1973 before Lindsay's next feature film, *O Lucky Man* was made. Arthur played three roles, Mr Duff, Charlie Johnson and Dr Munda, and he won a British Film Academy Award for best supporting actor.

Malcolm McDowell wrote the screenplay with David Sherwin, who had written *If . . . .* He also played the lead part of Mick Travis, the same character he'd played in *If . . .* – the film showed what happened to him afterwards. Alan Price wrote the score, Ondricek was the cameraman again and Lindsay's cast included many of his 'regulars'. Michael Medwin played two parts, the Captain and Dickie Belminster. In *If . . .* Mona Washbourne had given a most unusual and sensual performance as matron, now she too played multiple parts, Sister Hallet, an usher and a neighbour. Lindsay collected delightful old ladies. He was delightful himself: *agent provocateur*, I think whenever I see a photograph of him in blouson jacket and cap.

Meanwhile Arthur's theatre work was flourishing and he was fit and slim – for him – and all the troubles of Manchester were behind him. Yet he took happy pills and vitamin B2 injections and had long bouts of bad temper.

It was as if, for all the pushing and shoving and striving, he couldn't move his own career along fast enough.

The mid-sixties saw a fashion, started by the revivals of *Love For Love* and *The Recruiting Officer* by Olivier's National Theatre at the Old Vic, for dusting off Restoration Comedies. Arthur scored a big personal success in the role of Sir Davy Dunce in *The Soldier's Fortune* by Thomas Otway at the Royal Court Theatre.

The production was directed by Peter Gill. Sheila Hancock and Wallas Eaton and Arthur Lowe took the leading parts.

> There is plenty of historical interest in the plays of Thomas Otway and if we do not see them more often it is probably not that they are poor plays but that they seemed indecent to the taste of an earlier day . . .
>
> *Philip Hope-Wallace, Guardian*

I remember a line which went something like, 'mustering a dish of roaring, ranting whores . . . ', all good rumbustious stuff. Arthur played the cuckold of the piece and one critic obviously went on the wrong night:

> Arthur Lowe began shakily as Sir Davy Dunce, looking at first as if he was not sure that he had got into the right theatre in the right play . . .
>
> *Sunday Times*

But to quote all the good crits that Arthur had for his performances in *The Soldier's Fortune,* would take too long. Here are two, and the second one is especially potent, when you see who it's by:

Arthur Lowe as Sir Davy Dunce . . . turns out a performance such as I can't remember in a Restoration comedy since Cyril Ritchard played in *The Relapse*. Sir Davy is an archetypal Restoration husband, a rich, proud, silly old man, born to be cuckolded; Mr Lowe gives him a pink pig's face between a King Charles II wig and a snuff-stained snuff-brown suit, and plays the part as freshly as if it were something from a very good current comedy . . .

Mr Lowe can speak the most insignificant line with such a point that it gets a laugh; and at the end, where he is humiliated beyond all permissible bounds, his pathos is all the deeper for being expressed in comic terms. A marvellous performance.

B.A. Young, Financial Times

. . . Arthur Lowe brings to the part of Sir Davy a lightness of touch, a felicity, an innocence . . .

Tom Stoppard, Plays and Players

And I must just give you one more, because it's my personal favourite:

As Sir Davy Dunce, Arthur Lowe is very funny indeed. With his spaniel wig, his over-ripe voice and his family-doctor repertoire of reassuring noises, he ranges with unflagging animation from threatening manfully to 'sally out like Tamburlaine upon the Trojan horse', to subsiding, with dropping jaw, like a bewildered turbot.

91

Bernard Miles wrote from the Mermaid Theatre on Puddle Dock:

> Dear Mr Lowe,
> I must write a word of congratulation for your Davy Dunce which I saw last night. It's really quite superb, reminding me not a little of Hay Petrie, the finest classical low comedian of the past 40 years – did you ever see him? I hope you will come and do a play at the Mermaid soon – I will try and find something really good. Once again congratulations and thanks!
> Yours sincerely, Bernard Miles

While Bernard Miles was scratching his head looking for a new part for Arthur, Arthur got happily involved in a revival of one of Miles's old shows.

It was 1967. Swindley was dead, if not yet buried, and Arthur went off and enjoyed a long tour together with Joan in *Lock Up Your Daughters.* It was adapted by Bernard Miles from Henry Fielding. The music was by Laurie Johnson and the lyrics by Lionel Bart. The musical director was Jack Peberdy, but most of all I remember the orchestra, the Betty Smith Quintet. I spent my school holidays on tour with them and had my eyes opened. I had assumed, because everybody was called darling, that they all got on like a house on fire. When I told the ASM that my mother said that one of the men sang flat, the person in question poked his nose up to mine and hissed,

'Tell your mother that if I sing flat she looks like a fucking gargoyle.' It was quite a shock and probably a salutary corrective for a fourteen-year-old. Then we were back home, I was back at school and Dad was back at the Royal Court with *Marya,* a Russian play from the thirties by Isaac Babel translated by Christopher Hampton.

> The play is not all sadness and sorrow, Arthur Lowe, formerly of TV's *Coronation Street,* sees to that. He plays two roles – a crippled soldier and later a workman scrubbing floors. He makes some trenchant and amusing comments on people and the state of the world in general. Delivered in a slight Lancashire accent, they are so typically British, and so very welcome.
> *Staff writer for the Manchester Evening News*

Soap-stigma. Arthur would sit at the breakfast table in his dressing gown and zip-up bootees, yet-to-shave, and read through a pile of Durrant's press cuttings.

'Roll up! Roll up! You'll want to see this! You've seen one of the actors on the telly. The Russians never saw it but get down to the theatre and see Swindley being a Red Army veteran – Christ!'

I didn't quote one of the reviews for the Otway play because I didn't want to spoil your mood, but read it now, it was in the Daily Mirror:

> MR SWINDLEY SETS THE PACE
> If you've got a hammy role, serve it up with a bit of mustard, and like as not you'll convince the audience they are present at a banquet.
> That's what Arthur Lowe does in *The Soldier's Fortune* at the Royal Court Theatre.
> Mr Lowe, better known to TV viewers as *Coronation Street*'s Leonard Swindley, has a

sense of comic timing, which I wish others in the cast could achieve. When he is on stage in Thomas Otway's Restoration comedy, all is well.

As his wife, ever eager to leap into bed with her lover, Sheila Hancock has some amusing moments; as does Wallas Eaton in the part of Sir Jolly Jumble.

But this slowly spun out tale needs more pace – and a bit more ham all round.

Arthur Thirkell

Henry Livings knew just how Arthur felt:

I was just saying hello to him after the show and he was pulling on his pants and two or three lads, very well meaning, barged in and said 'Hey up Arthur, you didn't do bad tonight, did you?' And I mean, God knows how they had got past the stage door, but it was a nightmare.

Christmas came and an unusual panto at the Royal Court, another Russian play, *The Dragon* by Yevgeny Schwartz:

In the foyer the cashier bravely distributes tickets from the depths of a dragon's head: the programmes convert into dragon-masks; the stage is framed by winking, multi-coloured fairylights. At the back of the stage is a large screen onto which are projected exquisite, dreamlike pictures, evocative of the changing moods – two blood-red splayed feet for the dragon (one animal, one human) soft drifting leaves for the lovers, silhouettes of a steepled, domed town. Magic fills the stage . . .

Hampstead Express

Arthur Lowe is superb as the rascally Mayor, half Krushchev, half West Riding tycoon . . .

The Tablet

It was a very happy Christmas and it was the end of Phase One and we were on the eve of Phase Two. The next year, 1968, was to bring three dramatic changes: one of which was for our unimaginable financial good, one which seemed like a good idea at the time, and one which was sadly destructive but somehow inevitable.

5
'Man of the hour'
1968–1971

LET'S do the sadly destructive one first. When Joan and Arthur had moved to 33 and 35 Pavilion Road, 'The Pavilion' they called this rambling bohemian flat, they had taken on the remaining lease. It was for about ten years which seemed like a long time at the start, but even ten years comes around quite quickly and the lease was not renewed because the building was part of a big development plan. Now they had only a year to run, and there was pressure being put on them to make other arrangements. Later, the house was demolished: a Holiday Inn now stands in its place. Joan, particularly, loved the Pavilion, and she didn't give a toffee after that went. I've met people who are dearly attached to houses since but none like her: she was like a cat. She properly existed only in that time and place.

Then there was the thing that seemed like a good idea at the time. Arthur, pragmatic, looked around for something new. One Sunday morning they were sitting as they did in summer, in deck chairs on the roof garden surrounded by flowers and the Sunday Times and lubricated with Black Velvet – that sure-fire fifty-fifty mix of Guinness and Champagne – and one of them saw this advertisement:

HOUSEBOAT

Either £120 P.W. income from £2000 investment by purchase of this beautifully fitted ex-steam yacht, or ideal permanent home. The vessel is capable of accommodating 10 in comfort. At present moored London, but alternative mooring available Norfolk Broads. Constructed from 2' Burma teak, sheathed in copper, the hull is practically maintenance free. For further details contact the Sole Agent.

We all set off in the drop-head Daimler to have a look. We went out along the Cromwell Road to the west, Dad on his cushion commanding two lanes. It was mild and sunny and we were off on one of our little adventures. When we arrived at Cubitt's Yacht Basin, near the rowing club at Chiswick, we followed a narrow track through luxuriant and overgrown bushes down to a stagnant basin the surface of which was covered in a bright green algae.

Various houseboats were arranged higgledy-piggledy around the perimeter, and old couples and young couples and a yawning dog shared the peace of the afternoon.

'There she is,' we shouted in chorus. 'That must be her, mustn't it?'

A big, characterful vessel lay with her nose to the bank with a rickety gangway slung to the shore. She had a deckhouse and a wheel and a funnel. There were some plant pots scattered about and a general air of comfortable dereliction.

Dad went off to find the Sole Agent,

'Sounds pretty fishy.'

Mum nervously bit her thumbnail, obviously with a 'feeling' coming on. When we went on board and the agent pushed back the squeaking hatch, we were met by a pungent smell which has now permeated my skin and clothes, my life, and which should I ever smell it to my dying day will bring me winging back to 'Amazon'. To landsmen I suspect it is an unsavoury smell, comprising bilge-water, coal dust and diesel oil, but to boat people it is a nostalgic, evocative thing recalling in an instant those happy sea-borne days, away from the complications of shore life, lived out on an elemental plane of self-sufficiency and self-reliance.

This was Arthur's romantic vision. But more often than not, it had to be consummated in the form of on-board dinner parties where the guests were asked to turn off lights to conserve the power, not to wash their hands under a running tap to conserve water, and to conduct themselves as economically as they possibly could, even though the vessel never left the security of the jetty. Colin Bean – who played Private Sponge – did handsome little signs to this effect which Arthur pinned up everywhere: PASSENGERS ARE RESPECTFULLY REMINDED THAT FUEL AND WATER ARE VITAL TO THE VESSEL'S SAFETY AND WELL-BEING. PLEASE TURN OFF LIGHTS AND CONSERVE WATER WHEREVER POSSIBLE.

This log book smells of her now as I turn the pages in search of a distillate of that first summer that we had the boat.

In the cabins things were dingy. There was a sinister, *Marie Céleste* air of a place only recently, or maybe not quite completely, deserted. A cloak of madness hung, dimming the light from the hatchway. Undeterred, and even as we looked around in those first few minutes, Arthur was making lists of things that would have to be done.

The purchase of the boat was clearly a foregone conclusion and no doubt accounted for the imbecile grin on the agent's face. I too was very happy, for houses, however rambling, hedged me in, and here I could see myself at once at home. Joan moved around in a trance, certain from the start. It was Sunday, so when we left there had been no exchange of money – only promises that arrangements at the bank would be made in the morning. I didn't sleep too well that night, terrified that my parents' better judgement would prevail and that they would not go through with it.

But they did. Just two days later the document was drawn up and signed, and very soon after that our friends the Shines came down to the boat, and together we carried load after load of detritus to a bonfire that smouldered away for ten days. The old boat rose in the water by an inch every day that we worked. Carpenters were engaged, but the more they did, the more it seemed would need to be done. Further arrangements were made at the bank; late nights around the dining table with graph paper and animated discussion became the norm. We were not agreed as to where this was all leading. Arthur had some very grand ideas, based perhaps on his experiences aboard the 'Queen Mary'. My mother more realistically, had set a target of civilised bohemia at Chiswick. To Joan, the wheel, at that early stage at least, would make a handy thing for sweet peas to cling to. In Arthur's mind he was already lashed to it, having sent the rest of us below while he saw us safely through the storm and the night. Probably for no other reason than that it was two boys vs. one girl, refurbishment of the old craft was steered firmly towards a second wind of sea voyaging, at considerable expense and against considerable odds.

Meanwhile the third thing had happened, the one that was to be for our unimaginable financial good. A chap called Jimmy Perry had written a script about a few Home Guard characters: a self-important sergeant, an old veteran, and a stupid boy. Jimmy didn't just come out of nowhere as some people imagine. He, like Arthur, had been in Army Entertainments, he'd been at Butlins, trained at RADA, had worked for years in rep. He had actually thought out the Home Guard idea around Arthur and Bob Dorning after watching them in *Pardon The Expression*, a successful sitcom, which also starred Betty Driver. It was a spin-off from the Swindley character; Jimmy and his wife thought Arthur, especially, was very good in it. Jimmy approached David Croft in the car park at Television Centre. The story has become a legend now: Croft, who was an established producer at the BBC, was very fond of flash cars. He was tinkering with his car when Perry, nervous and feeling at a disadvantage, asked him if he'd read his script. Croft wears large spectacles and you can't always make out his eyes behind them.

'Excuse me,' Perry said.

A journey of a thousand miles begins with just one step. Together they developed the idea, Jimmy the one with the endless stream of naive ideas and the passion for truth, David the one with the know-how. They had trouble getting it past the big guns at the BBC – it was called *The Fighting Tigers* then – who weren't convinced that a show that laughed at Britain's finest hour could be a success.

David and Jimmy worked out the thing about the grammar-school Captain and the public-school Sergeant; Jimmy wanted Arthur for the part of Mainwaring. Thorley Walters had been put forward for the part. He'd been playing Sir Joshua Hoot QC in *Misleading Cases* which Michael Mills was producing. Michael Mills had quite a hand in the casting of *Dad's Army,* and it's a well-known fact of the business that producers can only remember actors they have seen in the last few days. Thorley Walters would have been fine in the part, but it's hard for us to imagine now that anybody other than Arthur could have done it. Jimmy didn't have any say in those early days but he just kept re-iterating the words 'Arthur Lowe' and eventually David Croft went with him to see Arthur in *Baked Beans And Caviar* at Windsor. No fault of the cast, it wasn't terribly good, but slowly Jimmy won David round. Even then he wasn't in. There was a cultural obstacle for Arthur – or rather for the establishment. He hadn't done much television for the BBC; he'd got Granada written all the way through.

'We don't know him do we? Isn't he up North doing *Jubilee Road* or something?'

The casting is said to have driven the show forward. John Laurie's part of Fraser, a dour Scot, ex-Royal Navy cook turned undertaker, and Arnold Ridley's part of Godfrey, an incontinent old gent, neither were originally conceived as such major parts.

Jimmy and Arthur got on very well. They shared a common experience in rep – which bonds actors like nothing else, gives them instant street-cred – and they shared a common source for many of their comedy routines, Will Hay. Croft and Perry were to have a great future because they didn't write about sofas:

> *Dad's Army* had the enclosed atmosphere I like, when you have men in a trapped environment. That way you don't get involved in family matters. I've written 450 scripts and not one of them has been a domestic.
> *David Croft in Sunday Telegraph, April 1995*

They went for a big cast too, so they had some space in which to develop the individual characters and the sub plots. Everything they went on to write – *It Ain't Half Hot Mum, 'Allo 'Allo, Hi-De-Hi!* – had big casts, none of it dwelt on domestic matters and it will all be immortal, preserved not just as an example of what is good, but as a whole discrete era of British Comedy. They have become giants.

*

Long avenues of trees, clean light, flat fields and straight roads – rural France. The window down and the mid-day sun – even now, in December – warm on my bare forearm. Here and there a seemingly deserted village, neat houses down each side of the road, ten points if you spot a nun on a moped with a baguette tied to the rack. A tractor in a field, and you couldn't say if it was two hundred yards or half-a-mile away. I must focus on this time in Arthur's life if I'm ever to escape from this walk with the zombies.

*

It means so little to me – *Dad's Army* – and so much to everybody else. Eighty-odd episodes – so many that the same number is never reported twice – all so funny, all stacked up wobbly on a plinth, the dizzy heights of comedy to which we're told Ben Elton might aspire. A pile of newspaper cuttings ankle-deep on my office floor, every new comedy writer blasted with the critic's flame-thrower, or held up in tweezers for comparison:

> . . . it must be asked: why are so many of the new comedies so unfunny? Unfortunately there is no single simple answer. Take *The Thin Blue Line*. It seems that creator Ben Elton is an admirer of *Dad's Army* and wanted to create . . .
>
> *Christopher Dunkley, Financial Times*

> When you think about the funniest moments, you probably don't dwell too long on recent programmes. You're more likely to recall *Dad's Army* . . .
>
> *Colin Cameron, Sunday Post*

The thickest folder of all is the one with the repeat-fee statements. Thank you Jimmy, David, Equity, God. And yet I feel nothing.

I laugh like everybody else because it's so funny, I love it. I have loads of episodes on tape, all neatly labelled. Our little girl demands them,

'Daddy, put on Captain Mango. I want Captain Mango.'

But I don't see my father, I seem to see a shadow, like a light show on the wall.

Most of the anecdotes linked to Arthur's time on *Dad's Army* relate to trousers, the lavatory, his chronic lateness, his inability to learn his lines and his delusions of grandeur. There is a lot of Arthur in Mainwaring, newspaper writers delight in pointing out. Well, there would be because David and Jimmy wrote to the characters, for ten years, so some fusion took place between actor and character.

Arthur thought that,

'Anybody could get a laugh if they pissed into the pit. But it wouldn't be the right laugh.'

And it was undoubtedly his influence which kept the show so clean, cited many times as one of its major virtues. It is said that written into his contract was a clause stating that no bombs would be put down his trousers. In the same black and white episode in which Jonesy gets a bomb put in a sensitive place, episode number 4, trousers are featured when the uniforms first arrive. When Wilson and Mainwaring find the buttons are at the side, they realise they've been sent trousers meant for the ATS, but happily both men do all the trouser business on the far side of the bank's counter and we are left to do the mental donkey-work for ourselves. The rule is upheld.

They all stayed at The Bell and at The Anchor at Thetford when they did the outside stuff and travelled to the location in a bus. Arthur was invariably the last to emerge from the hotel, with everybody else, from David Croft to thirteenth wardrobe assistant, drumming their fingers or burying their heads in the crossword. When Arthur missed the bus altogether, Jimmy Perry used to wait for him and they'd drive together in Jimmy's Beetle. Arthur confided one day that,

'These early morning starts play havoc with my lavatorial arrangements.'

Jimmy bought him a packet of All-Bran. 'It's like eating the stuffing of a mattress,' commented Arthur, but it did the trick. However, it is Godfrey who emerges – in the Columbia Pictures feature film – from the unusually located cliff-top Gents to take up his place in the haunting tableau; the one image from the film that can never fade.

The most enduring of these anecdotes relates to Arthur never knowing his lines. It is only natural, I suppose, that people should fix on the apparent anomaly that one of the finest actors of modern times should have difficulty learning his lines. John le Mesurier hinted, after a frustrating rehearsal, that Arthur might take his script home and learn his part. Arthur looked at him for a moment, the pause held in the air like a tennis player about to serve, 'I don't want a thing like that in my home.'

Arthur's likeness to the Little French General – Hodges' line typically, 'Alright, Napoleon?' – surfaced often. At home he talked of Moses and Montgomery, of the man with the money calling the tune. Getting on the location bus one day some cheerful soul well down in the pecking order called out,

'Morning Arfur!' as the gallant Captain stepped aboard.

Sitting down beside Harold Snoad, Arthur looked at his director and friend, 'Arthur? That'll have to change.'

I wondered sometimes if he had been bullied at school, certainly he was by his mother. For me to watch his merciless treatment of Wilson in 'The Honourable Man' is chilling. Mainwaring is a small man, a terrier, and his cruel bite nearly cripples Wilson. That episode is the kernel, and if I can take only one with me when I go then that will be it.

*

The narrow band of the road controls my life, and while I just go on like this I don't really need to address the future nor come to terms with the past. But journey's end will come, the goods will be delivered.

Facing a cold future of just 256 digitised colours, half the output in cartoon to save on actors, animatronics performing Shakespeare, Photoshop humanoforms singing *Carmen*, will we bury *Dad's Army* in a time capsule for future generations to find? *Dad's Army* will endure: it represents the deserted front of human kindness, 'The Battle of Godfrey's Cottage'. When I see an episode now, protected by a calloused heart, I get a pleasant little surprise like a cool breeze springing up on a blistering day, or a ray of sunshine warming your back in winter. Delighted, I find it's all about gentle human values.

Also it represents everything that is quintessentially English in an entertainment medium that is increasingly in the American or Australian idiom. So many people strangely attempting to adopt the attitudes of younger nations.

Social structure and good form swapped for a classless, faceless society and directionless independent action. Understatement exchanged for shouted hyperlative. Quaint eccentricity shunned for clonism. Boyishness outgrown and displaced by street-wise. Enthusiasm displaced by cool. But truthfully, kewl is shallow and at the heart of the matter is the sad fact that we wish we could have the old days back, but we've given them away. Now we turn our dishes to the sky, as if in supplication to the satellites. Trusting them to beam us vintage comedy, like beacons of hope.

But the way lies forward. Soon I shall be pointing this ageing Scania at the Blanc, roaring up and up into the dark night. Into a long dark tunnel from which I will emerge into the bright sunshine sparkling off the new snow on the Italian slopes.

*

As before with *Coronation Street*, the making of *Dad's Army* did not occupy the whole year. There was plenty of time for other things and this is how many of the team went along, refreshed by a variety of other work they would return to rehearsals for *Dad's Army* like a group of sporting guns gathering for the glorious twelfth.

The first year, Arthur appeared in *Home And Beauty* with Olivier's still National Theatre. Dad was thrilled to be invited to play there, and proud as Punch. But his cheeky side could not be hidden, and at home he did cruel impersonations of Larry Olivier to entertain my Mum. The critics didn't approve the choice of play, or enjoy the production, or many of the performances. But they loved Arthur:

> It is 50 years since Somerset Maugham wrote *Home And Beauty*, now revived at the National Theatre, and it cannot truthfully be said that age has sat lightly on it. The play's funniest moments come in the final act when all three [a war-widow, her second husband, and, embarrassingly, her first husband returned] are advised by a dubious solicitor, played with arch assurance by Arthur Lowe, about the techniques for proving desertion, cruelty and adultery in the divorce courts. As for the rest of it, in spite of some spirited comic acting on the

parts of Geraldine McEwan, Robert Stephens and Robert Lang, this predictable farce is likely to elicit more yawns than guffaws.

Evening Standard, 9 October 1968

There is nothing much wrong with *Home And Beauty;* but bringing so many resources – human and technical – to bear upon it is rather like asking Joe Davis to give up billiards for marbles . . . There was a marvellous supporting performance from Arthur Lowe – as fruity as an orchard in autumn. Frank Dunlop's production was clean and well-paced, but here, too, one felt that it was child's play.

Hugh Leonard, Plays and Players

Anthony Easterbrook, the theatre's General Manager, wrote to Arthur:

I have a note from Sir Laurence that he particularly desires that you should be paid your appearance money for Friday, 17 January. I am told that he takes the view that it is impossible to find that chap Plinge, and can therefore only assume that the enclosed cheque should come to you.

Please accept it with our best wishes and thank you for the many delightful performances you gave in *Home And Beauty.*

Arthur did *If* . . . but he also appeared in a film written by Spike Milligan and John Antrobus, *The Bed Sitting Room.* The director was Richard Lester, who had directed

Hard Day's Night in 1964 and *Help!* the following year. The plot meandered around strange mutant events after 'the bomb'; Arthur and his family, played by Mona Washbourne, Rita Tushingham and Richard Warwick, live on the Circle Line and eat by raiding chocolate machines. Eventually Arthur mutates into a parrot and goes and sits on Ralph Richardson who has mutated into a wardrobe and they are both inside someone else, I think, who has changed into a bed sitting room. Halliwell's verdict:

> Arrogantly obscure fantasy, a commercial flop which kept its director in the wilderness for four years . . .

It had a large cast, and some well-known names. I remember a visit to a location; a windy common some-where, sitting in a caravan with my father and Michael Hordern. We looked out of the window as Peter Cook and Dudley Moore floated by in the basket of a hot air balloon. It was anchored to a Land Rover by a long rope.

'Have you got a knife?' Arthur asked.

They were all pleased, and just a little surprised – Jimmy must have felt elated, and proud – when it was announced that there would be a second series of *Dad's Army,* to be recorded in October and November. It had touched a spot in the nation's heart, had hit the right balance of comedy and nostalgia, gags and pathos. When it ran to a third series, kicking off with 'The Armoured Might of Lance Corporal Jones', recorded in the May of 1969, they were ecstatic.

That year David Croft – a long-established theatre producer before he ever joined the BBC – put on *Ann*

Veronica. Adapted by Croft from the H.G. Wells novel, the show went to Brighton and Coventry before opening at the Cambridge. Croft's career-long friend Cyril Ornadel wrote the score, and it brought Arthur great happiness meeting with this old friend from his past, too. Cyril had been the musical director on *Call Me Madam* and now Arthur was back up there, singing and dancing, and loving every minute of it. Cyril wrote to him:

> Dear Arthur, what a thrill it has been to work with you again after all these years – thank you for a really funny 'Ramage' [the character Arthur played in *Ann Veronica*] and for your magnificent rendering of the numbers – no matter how many times I watch you, you always make me roar with laughter! I wish you an enormous personal success – with my grateful thanks, as ever, Cyril.

Unfortunately, it wasn't to be a success for anybody. The first thing that happened was that Dorothy Tutin quit, saying her voice wasn't strong enough: an unpropitious start in a poor climate. Six musicals had failed in the West End already that year, and *Ann Veronica* came off after just eight weeks. It was a particularly hard knock for David Croft, who had put five years into it. The exact losses weren't made public, but they were thought to be around £60,000.

There's really no patriotism in some critics; we're talking employment here, and not just the cast and the orchestra, the stagehands and the barmen and the cleaners. It's about Americans and Japanese coming to the West End and eating in the restaurants, taking a black cab, staying in a hotel. Getting their shoes polished by a boot-boy. It's about the flowers that will come from the country in the night, be bought and sold at Covent Garden and delivered to the hotel by a man who drives a van and has a family in Wapping. This is about London, about Britain.

These aren't my words, these are Arthur's. The critics have precious little respect sometimes, and when Dad read crits like the ones for *Ann Veronica* I know it made his blood boil. I know the other side of the coin is the maintaining of standards, but we're not talking about fringe theatre or flash-in-the-pan television soap personalities in panto, we're talking about David Croft and Cyril Ornadel, masters.

> One had dimly hoped that . . . the musical might catch something of the aggressive crusading spirit of the early socialists, but instead we are offered a succession of pastel coloured romantic numbers interspersed with the occasional, seriously under-attended protest meeting . . . For the rest there is a besetting ordinariness about both Cyril Ornadel's music and David Croft's lyrics.
>
> *Michael Billington, The Times*

I'm not surprised when I read in the same piece that Arthur kept his end up:

> Two performances help to save the evening from total mediocrity. One is that of the admirable Arthur Lowe, red-faced and downright, as a lecherous business man . . . Hy Hazell, brisk

and bowlerhatted, also lends the part of a militant suffragette a booming, boisterous élan.

Downright what? I wonder. It was a lovely show, I saw it in Coventry before it came into town. David Croft, years later on *Desert Island Discs*, said of Arthur, 'He came on like a lion.'

Arthur was now in some demand as a television personality. He abhorred this concept – points scored by the great unwashed – and feared more than anything losing his identity as an actor. He was in constant demand to appear for interviews and guest-spots on shows like *Charlie Chester, Woman's Hour, Desert Island Discs, Quiz Ball, The Cilla Black Show, The Tommy Cooper Show*.

He acquired a reputation as an after-dinner speaker and this brought a number of invitations to the Guild Halls and so on in London. Amusingly, this pomp and splendour gave him great pleasure, and I would say that in the main he was really honoured to be a guest at these things. It was tradition and patriotism at its best. Charitable work, on the other hand, was not really his thing; in the main he confined his activity to the RNLI, the Lifeboat. See though this lovely little note from Arthur Askey in 1974 about the arrangements to celebrate his 70th birthday:

Dear Arthur,
I am more than delighted to hear that you have accepted the invitation to the Variety Club Luncheon on October 17th. Vive les Arthurs!

Would you be a nice feller and say a few words please? They tell me you make a smashing speech and I'd like to hear it on my great day. Only three or four minutes would do – as long as you'll get on your feet.

Shall look forward to meeting up with you again – meantime

All good wishes.

Yours aye.

It seems too he could be persuaded to go along to fêtes and so on if the name was big enough, or the political persuasion correct. Ted Heath was quite a fan, and Arthur in turn was a Heath follower. He even got his mugshot on an 'Into Europe' poster once – well-known faces that supported Europe sort of thing. This letter is out of place chronologically, but it's on-topic:

23rd October 1978

Dear Arthur Lowe

Many thanks for your note of the 20th October and I am delighted to hear you and your wife hope to come to Sidcup on Saturday, 18th November.

I am sure there will be no difficulty over transport. It is very good of you to fit this engagement into your busy programme.

With best wishes,

Yours sincerely,
Edward Heath

He was offered – and took – an immense amount of commercial work: Barclays Bank, Lyons Pie Mix, Shell Oil, The Furniture Show, Florida Orange Juice, Spam,

Bournevita, Walls Ice Cream, the Butter Council and Brooke Bond Tea.

'The man's got no dignity,' John Laurie said, 'Pay him a thousand pounds and he'd dress up as a monkey.'

The fee for an episode of *Dad's Army* had been around a hundred and fifty pounds, and by 1971 it was up around the six hundred pound mark. One commercial paid, typically, a thousand pounds.

With the year drawing to a close he went with Jimmy Beck to BBC Leeds to record Henry Livings's adaptation of *The Government Inspector*. The Yorkshire Post reported in a predictable style:

> These household TV personalities had not travelled to Leeds to act before the cameras. They were parading their talents for radio microphones . . .
>
> *Michael Colbert, Yorkshire Post*

It must have been frustrating for Henry and the other members of the cast, Geoffrey Wheeler and John Sharp. Jimmy Beck was a cracking actor and I'd have loved to read some constructive comment.

Columbia Pictures came forward with a budget and the next year saw them making the *Dad's Army* film. Everybody except the two veterans of British films, John Laurie ('Doomed!') and John le Mesurier ('Are you sure this is wise?') were excited at the prospect. Arthur is said to have behaved rather badly, like a star. One of the old Shepperton hands whispered a complaint to that effect in John le Mesurier's ear, something about 'Kitty's revolver'. John looked into the middle distance and gave that secretive, wry smile as he tried to work out just how his

115

friend came to get that nickname. He knew about the revolver; Arthur had gone off to Woolworths himself, to try and buy a plastic one – he had found the replica too heavy. But Kitty? No-one knew how Arthur earned that.

Shepperton technicians weren't the only people to think that Arthur could be grit in life's vaseline. The team appeared as guests on *The Morecambe And Wise Show*.

'Do you think this is wise?' was Eric's line. Arthur, ad-libbing, topped it with,

'No this is Wise, the one with the short, fat hairy legs.'

And got the laugh. He probably hadn't done any more than scan the script in the taxi on the way there, and there he was, winging his way and getting the laughs. Eric trapped him in the corridor, half Arthur's height again, he started poking a finger into his chest.

'I do the laughs on this show, don't you forget that.'

The put-down wouldn't have had much effect. Arthur was always back on his feet, ready for another go.

He scored a big personal hit, one that meant a lot to him, in the film *The Ruling Class*. Peter O'Toole played the lead, Jack, 14th Earl of Gurney, and Arthur played a drunken, anarchic butler (not the only time he was cast in such a role). When Arthur and Joan – Joan had a part in the film too, she played Nurse Brice – arrived at the hotel there was a note on the their dressing table: 'Blessed are they that steal the best parts. POT.'

It turned out to be very true: for all the great lines Peter O'Toole had – such as, 'How do you know you're God?' 'When I pray I find I'm talking to myself.' – it was Arthur who stole the film. It was a very good time, they hit it off quite extraordinarily well, Joan too. The film was produced by Jules Buck and Jack Hawkins. They all came down to the 'Amazon' and ate and drank very well; Jules's crazy, brash thank-you for the evening was to offer Arthur a blank cheque for the boat. Peter O'Toole was nominated for an Academy Award for his part in *The Ruling Class,* but that year it went to Marlon Brando for *The Godfather.* It was the nearest Arthur got to big pictures and it's something he'd dearly have liked to have more of. He came home and did a few more Spam commercials and recorded *Parsley Sidings* on radio with Ian Lavender.

Joanie had enjoyed having a part in *The Ruling Class,* she'd given up too many years to bringing up her two boys. She had also gone off and done something on her own, William Douglas Home's play *The Reluctant Debutante* at Dundee Rep. A letter she wrote to Arthur while she was away is the first evidence of a problem that later became devastating:

Friday 1 a.m.

Oh my darling,
I am certainly 'feeling the pull of the old place' as Mick Murrell would say – I can't really be bothered to do the last two performances (particularly as I've already been <u>paid</u>) – oh how seriously these children take their work! I just want to come HOME to <u>you</u>!! Golly, I never realised just how hopeless it would be without you. Of course I've been spoiled, mostly by thirty commercial travellers, – Donald [friend] is so shy that he isn't really much help – and of course I've been happy in the dressing room with the girls – but it's just not <u>important</u> enough – it is if they laugh like drains – like on Wednesday then it's marvellous – but audiences

are such wets – they really only deserve television – I'm glad I've done it – if only to find
out that it isn't enough!

Soon be Sunday now! Longing to hold you
close. Must try to sleep, but I'm so excited –
goodnight, my Tim, so glad you like your
lamps,

Oodles and oodles, Pony.

They are playing 'Pennsylvania 6-5000' which
of course makes it even worse!

Amongst all the thousands of newspaper cuttings that I
have looked through there are none about Joan's time at
Dundee. It makes me suspicious that she may not have
received a good write-up. As Godfrey's sister Dolly, no
real problem. Anything more substantial and – whoops.
Her performances were actually quite charming, but they
were, frankly, locked in a time warp from which even
Spock could not have calculated an exit. It put Arthur in
a very tricky position.

He did a lot of other television work at that time too,
*Cuckoo In The Nest, Plunder, Dirty Work, Rookery Nook,
She Follows Me About*. This series of Ben Travers's
Aldwych farces, broadcast from the theatre complete
with live audience, co-starred Richard Briers. Arthur's
sharp nose for billing nearly brought the two of them –
who got on fine in every other respect – to blows.
Eventually they agreed to take alternate weeks at the top
of the bill which was fine until Dicky was looking
around for an audience admission ticket – he kept one
from everything he did as a souvenir. To his considerable distress, he could only find one which had Arthur's

name first. I remember tears rolling down my father's cheeks when he related the story at home.

Ben Travers wrote to Arthur later in the year:

> I have waited until the end of the TV Series before writing to express my great admiration and gratitude to you for all the brilliant and amazingly versatile characterisations you provided and the uplift you gave to the whole undertaking. My word, how lucky I was to have had you in the shows.
>
> I need only say that if it should be my good fortune to try to cater for you again I will know who I am writing for and will do my best accordingly.

Not all of it was for the BBC. You might not think there'd be an anarchic side to the actor who played Mainwaring, but he hated to be pinned down. He did *The Last Of The Baskets* for Granada and *Doctor At Large* for LWT in which he played a general practitioner, Dr Maxwell. Arthur and the director of *Doctor At Large*, David Askey worked well together; and their association led to greater things at London Weekend later.

Last Of The Baskets – a sitcom written by John Stevenson and set in the rural North – is not a happy story. There could have been a part for Joan – she thought – and Arthur and his agent, Peter Campbell, tried, but Granada just wouldn't give it to her. Hermione Baddeley was offered it, but from the start Arthur was up to his old tricks of getting all her laughs written out. He behaved a bit as he'd done on *Pardon The Expression* when he caused Betty Driver to raise an eyebrow. Hermione

Baddeley, justifiably, became increasingly sour and left the series; Patricia Hayes took her place. Peter Campbell – we talked about it years later – was convinced that it was Joan, jealous, envious or whatever, manipulating Arthur, operating him almost like a puppet. *Last Of The Baskets* ran to two series but it wasn't the best thing he ever did. For Arthur it was scuppered from day one by Joan's input. For Peter it was particularly embarrassing because he represented both artists; he was also Hermione Baddeley's agent.

For Christmas there was a *Dad's Army Special,* 'The Battle of the Giants'. They had thirty-nine episodes of *Dad's Army* under their belts now, and it might be assumed that a jolly bunch of old chums turned up to throw together a biggy for Christmas. But in Jimmy Perry's words:

'The idea that they were one happy band was not true. They were the most irascible crowd.'

Sometimes I would go along to the recordings – I was seventeen now, and about to leave school to go into the Merchant Navy. Two episodes were usually recorded on the one night. Previously filmed location work was watched on overhead monitors by the audience as it was put down to tape, and in this way the storyline was kept in sequence and the entertainment was complete. One particular evening sticks in my mind, though I can't recall which episode. It was a great crack, with Felix Bowness doing the audience warm-up and Bill Pertwee maybe giving him a hand, and coach parties of fans arriving from far and wide, forsaking the safety of their living-rooms for a more electrifying experience. Harold Snoad, the assistant director, was on the floor, making his last minute preparations. Arthur and Clive Dunn, who played Jonesy, were just going through a particular bit of business, trying to get it to work. Clive would never do it the same way twice, and Dad, frustrated, came over to talk to me.

'He's not our sort, he's Variety, you know,' he said with a little crease around the eyes the only clue.

Dad was seriously envious of Clive's success with his single, *Grandad.* He tried to emulate this when he recorded *My Little Girl* on the EMI label but with no success at all. Not everything that he touched turned to gold.

Most of the team were real-life veterans, some of them in both world wars. Watching Arnold Ridley, born in 1896, shuffling about, it was hard for me to think of him as a young subaltern with the Somerset Light Infantry, fighting in the trenches in France in 1914, playing rugby and cricket for his county. He'd written *The Ghost Train,* my mother said – rather like Mrs Pike pointing out some virtue of Uncle Arthur to her daft son – but I had never seen a performance of the *The Ghost Train,* and I didn't know then that it had run for six hundred performances at the St Martin's Theatre. I didn't know – maybe Arthur didn't know – that Arnold had had money in films and lost the lot. I didn't know that he'd been in rep too at Birmingham and Plymouth, had appeared in loads of his own plays – he wrote about thirty, one or more a year except for during the Second World War because he'd gone back for another bash – and that six of his plays were made into films.

And John Laurie, sitting in a corner glowering at the last obstinate clue in The Times crossword, born in Dumfries in 1897, had served with the Hon. Artillery Company from 1916-1918. He, like grandfather Lowe, couldn't be drawn into conversation about his experiences in France, so horrific had they been.

Laurie's first appearance on the stage had been at the Lyceum, Dumfries, in 1921 in *What Every Woman Knows* by the author of *Peter Pan*. He was a Shakespearean actor and had a distinguished career which spanned nearly half a century before he ever began on *Dad's Army*. In films too he had a vast experience, I can count forty-nine films and my list may not be complete, starting with *Juno And The Paycock* in 1930 and ending with *The Prisoner Of Zenda* in 1979. Forty-nine years in movies. He was a gruff, abrasive man who spoke his mind. He knew *Dad's Army* to be well beneath him, ' . . . I end up becoming famous doing this crap!'

Asked by John le Mesurier who he thought had given the best Hamlet ever, he's said to have replied, 'Why me, laddie.' Not that John le Mesurier really deserved the title 'laddie'. He started in the theatre in 1932 when he joined the Fay Compton Studio of Dramatic Art. He was in rep at Edinburgh, Glasgow and Croydon – and in Hell, Hull and Halifax – and in 1939 he married his first wife, theatre manager June Melville. He signed on as an air-raid warden during the first year of the war, then he spent the better part of his service in India, where he refused an invitation to join the cast of a concert party being put on by gunner Perry. His first marriage was a war casualty. Demobbed and depressed at the prospect of returning to touring rep he looked for a way forward in films, he knocked on every door along Wardour Street. His first film appearance was in *Escape From Broadmoor*. Shortly after, he was in the rather more rewarding *Private's Progress*. He appeared in over fifty films, spanning thirty years.

John wasn't at all sure, either, about coming into *Dad's Army*. He was swung only by his friend Clive Dunn saying, 'If you'll do it, I'll do it.'

Wearing his habitually sad expression and cravat, he turned up at the first read-through wholly unconvinced as to the prospects for *Dad's Army*. The fee was rather poor and the rehearsal rooms in Acton really rather damp, don't you think?

The real laddie was of course Ian Lavender. He quickly made friends with John Laurie, who became a sort of mentor. Together they did The Times crossword.

I got a terrific buzz out of those evenings at the BBC, and to be in some small way connected with it gave it a special edge. I never felt that same strange reverence that came over me when I went backstage and onto the set of a play. But still the heat from the lights, and the trailing cables to the cameras, and the sense of clear purpose in everybody's actions, with David Croft in the control room – his twinkling eyes concealed behind his large spectacles – and Jimmy Perry sporting some outrageous fashion: it really was great to witness.

Everybody's spirits were high, they were working on a successful show. They hadn't yet had to face the fact that they had created a benign monster. As Ian Lavender put it in an interview:

> . . . It just happened. Like Topsy, it grew. The first three series were sort of small, medium, middling and then it went and flew to the top. That was a bit of a shock – suddenly we were everybody's property in the nicest sense, part of everybody's family.

6

'Art for Arthur's sake'

1972–1974

THEATRE *of Blood.* It might seem that we'd hit upon
an anomaly. Unless we think of Arthur's own words,
'. . . Took everything that was going, played whatever
had to be played . . . ', or John Laurie's, ' . . . Pay the
man a thousand pounds . . . '

Arthur – so like George Mainwaring in this – upheld
everything that was decent. On television. In the cinema
he felt he had a greater licence, protected by the rating
system. He'd have liked to see a rating system on television, a little 'X' or a 'U' permanently on in one corner of
the screen, not just for Granny but for the actors and the
management too. Also, I realise now, it is we who piously
link him with middle-class respectability, who patronise
him by saying we don't think he suits this part or that.

The plot of Anthony Greville-Bell's film gave Arthur
deep joy:

> A Shakespearean actor uses appropriate murder
> methods on the various critics who have ridi-
> culed his performances. *Halliwell's Film Guide*

Even if he did have to play Horace Sprout, one of the various critics, and have his head sawn off. Joanie had nightmares for months after she unwisely went to see the film. She'd wake sweating and scrabbling for Arthur's head to be sure it was still attached to his shoulders. Joan Hickson played Mrs Sprout: it was a great cast, Coral Browne, Diana Dors, Jack Hawkins, Michael Hordern, Robert Morley, Milo O'Shea, Dennis Price, Vincent Price, Diana Rigg, Eric Sykes and Peter Thornton among them. How could he have turned it down?

He worked again with Spike, this time on his film *Adolf Hitler: My Part In His Downfall,* but of more interest in that year was his return to the theatre, and a couple of interesting pieces of television work.

Just as Arthur would not commit himself for twelve months with the television companies, nor would he with the National Theatre. I'm told that, around this time, they would dearly have liked to have had him as a full-time member of the company.

I learnt more about this from a telephone call with Henry Livings. Henry, a heavy smoker all his life, had just had a puff on his ventilator and was particularly lucid.

> You probably know his phrase 'Art for Arthur's sake'. They [the management at the National Theatre] were awkward. Trying to tie him down to a bit of your contract artist in the National or the Royal Shakespeare. And I had written a musical version of *The Government Inspector* and I was trying to sell it to them. And they decided that this was the way to nail Arthur. What's that play? It's a grotesque play, and

Arthur had a very short scene in which he absolutely stole the reviews, and Olivier had no more wit, but that he sort of thought Arthur was a comedy actor. I never thought so, to try and replace him? So they were always looking for some way of blaming Arthur, because what he would do: he would go in, do a six weeks contract with the National and go right back to write yet another contract [with a television company]. It was his way of getting a rise!

Arthur himself said of all this, in the interview with Sheridan Morley:

> I've been asked to go back to the National when they move *The Tempest* into the new building next spring, and there's an idea that I might stay on there and do some Shaw and maybe a Pinero . . . I find it all a bit terrifying but I'd be a fool to turn it down out of funk.

Having been announced as Olivier's successor to run the National Theatre, Peter Hall's production of *The Tempest,* his first at the Old Vic, was in for particular scrutiny. The National Theatre was entering a new phase. Arthur was very proud to be a part of this enterprise, and unusually proud of the good reviews, which he normally treated with a certain nonchalance. He had jumped a high hurdle now, he felt. Michael Medwin, the producer of *If . . .* and *O Lucky Man!* wrote to him at the National:

> Many, many congratulations for your richly deserved award for *O Lucky Man!* and also for

your stunning personal reviews for *The Tempest*. I am off to New York shortly but hope to get in to see you at the National before I leave. Heartiest congratulations once again and here's to the next time.'

The first thing I note as I read through a pile of cuttings and the programme, carefully preserved by my mother, is that Professor John Russell Brown – newly appointed by Peter Hall as literary adviser to the National – had just published a plea to return Shakespeare to the actors and to restrict the influence of directors. Next I read:

The masque element appears to be a straight continuation of Mr Hall's exploration of baroque opera. To start with, artificiality is underlined with wafer-thin trees smothered in leaves like sequins and an orange sun suspended on two visible cords . . . when we reach the nuptials, a broken rainbow descends and the piece passes right over into opera as Iris delivers her prologue in melismatic recitative to a drone accompaniment . . .

Irving Wardle, The Times

I'm just getting into this, and thinking how incredibly clever it all is, and how I wish my Dad had had time to explain all these intricacies to me, when I read this:

Fortunately, comedy is in the safe hands of Arthur Lowe . . .

Frank Marcus, Sunday Telegraph

And I remember what Dad was like and how he would have divorced himself from all that.

'Oh, come away,' he'd say.

John Gielgud played Prospero. Arthur played Stephano, and Julian Orchard, Trinculo. Caliban was played by Denis Quilley. Irving Wardle wrote in Punch:

> Mr Orchard, a fleshy ladylike stooge in cap and bells, and Mr Lowe, a dangerous buffoon with powerful sense of his own dignity, make something very real of the sub-plot; and their enslavement of Caliban is genuinely disturbing.

When I read the play, I can imagine so clearly how he would have said the lines.

> STEPHANO. He that dies pays all debts: I defy thee. Mercy upon us!
> CALIBAN. Art thou afeard?
> STEPHANO. No, monster, not I.

Recently I spent a day in London on a combined mission. My first appointment was with James, Arthur's barber. He first started going to James when he had his shop on Knightsbridge. 'Maurice Varne', said the legend next to the striped barber's pole, and inside hung an oil painting of Maurice, a hairdresser from Belgium. Wonderful cut-glass bottles containing red, amber and blue lotions reflected, fragmented or sheared in bevelled looking-glass. Leather and chromium chairs from fifty years before were presided over by men in white coats, elbow raised to the intricate task of barbering generals and cabinet ministers, lords and actors, a bone comb or a glinting cut-throat in a dry hand. James, small, vigorous, Greek and with tiny dark shining eyes, would grip both your hands in a most genuine welcome,

'My dear. My dear Arthur, my dear Stephen. How very nice to see you.'

The whole scene re-iterated into infinity in the mirrors.

Now in a poky little room on the first floor of the Ritz Hotel, still with the painting of M. Varne dominating, and a photograph of the old place on Knightsbridge, a selection of the colourful bottles in just one of the cabinets, James is sitting alone, reading the paper. Rising, still vigorous for all his years, going a little blind, still the strong, neat hands in mine, the real greeting from the heart:

'Stephen, my dear. It is good to see you, it has been so long.'

We do the weather, and the prospects of the Government – a few governments have been and gone since first we met: I was, we think, six.

'You know I remember people by the shape of their heads,' I feel James's fingers passing over the back of my hair. 'Feeling your head now, it could be your dear father.'

There is a photograph of Arthur, a picture taken by Zoe Dominic, in a plain black cushion frame, in amongst other actors, military men and naval captains. I think if I paid attention I would recognise many of them, but my eyes are fixed on James, the bright light glinting off a little gold on a tooth and off those alert old eyes.

'It's not the same, Stephen, my dear. But what can we do? We must just keep trying.'

He shapes my beard to a naval style reminiscent of the Fleet Review; he spends a long time, perhaps an hour, but when I rise very little hair drops to the floor.

'Now you can face them with confidence,' he says holding up a hand mirror and brushing my suit with a long, soft brush with yellowing bristles, 'like your dear father.'

As I walk down the stairs I feel like going back and saying,

'When you see him, give him my love.'

My next appointment is with Alan Simpson; Ray Galton is – for very sad reasons – unable to come. A phone-call to Tessa le Barr – with them since she was a girl, now their agent, but more than just an agent, a friend, an accomplice – had fixed it up. Alan had suggested the Ritz, and it all fell so well into place. I find them – Alan huge and flashy beside Tessa, understated – sitting drinking wine when all about are drinking tea at the tea dance. At once I feel at home with this gentle giant and his small, bandaged friend. (I don't really understand, but it's something to do with tendons.) As at many of these meetings I am disadvantaged because it is assumed I know many things that are common knowledge to the business. Just as I might assume someone would automatically know that the tide would not turn until after lunch.

'No, I'm retired now, I gave all those years to it. Now I'm looking after Alan,' he says.

'How can you retire if you're a comedy writer? You can't just suddenly stop being funny.'

'Yes I can. I used to go in at nine o'clock, write scripts and then at five I'd go home. Not like Ray, he'd sit up in bed all night. Your father and Tony you know, they were both influenced . . . all that business in *Dad's Army,* you know I see Will Hay. They were both complex actors, straight actors speaking comedy, not comics.'

At the BBC's instigation, they'd re-worked the Tony Hancock scripts for Arthur to play the Hancock figure and Jimmy Beck to play the Sid James sidekick. They'd recorded one pilot and then Jimmy died. Arthur was not only heartbroken, he was highly superstitious, and he didn't want to go on with it. Alan shrugged his huge tartan shoulders, and you could see he thought it was a waste.

Later we all went out onto the street and got in different taxis. Back home, in my row of videotapes I preserve a gap, it's for *Bunclarke With An E,* as the series would have been called, a ray of hope that's never going to be beamed down to us.

Arthur was at his best now. Experience was in perfect balance with vigour and good humour, and during this period everything he did was spot on.

It was in this condition that he came back to the Royal Court Theatre to play Ben Jonson in Edward Bond's play, *Bingo.*

Theatre-goers and critics shuffled into the foyer on 14 August 1974 uncertain of what promise the evening held, Bond was inclined to write sermons, yet no-one wanted to miss John Gielgud playing Shakespeare, the man.

Telegrams from all over were pinned up in Arthur's dressing room:

GOOD LUCK TO RARE BEN JONSON = PETER HALL

= KEEP IT MANLY • = OTOOLE

DEAR ARTHUR CHEERS AND WELCOME BACK = LINDSAY +

We, the family, never went in to see him before the show, he really didn't like it. But we would go round to his dressing room after, and he would be there in his vest, cleaning off his make-up. It could be disturbing for the uninitiated to see him in the moments after he came off the stage, he was a man running at triple speed, surfing a long wave. We'd pour gin and tonics from a kit and, never more than fifteen minutes or so later, he'd be ready to go out to a restaurant or come home. Sometimes old friends would pop their heads around the door to say they'd loved it, and the best ones would be sympathetic and wouldn't stay. He would almost never agree to interviews of any kind, when he did he was highly selective:

> *Bingo*? It's a sequel to *The Tempest* really: remember Prospero's last speech? Clearly some kind of melancholia had set in to Shakespeare by then, and that's the mood of the man in Bond's play. I suppose if he were living nowadays they'd give him some happy pills and that would be that . . . but Bond's written about him in retirement, living at Stratford, being visited by some of the people from his past including me as Ben Jonson. We only have one scene, marvellous scene it is too: 10 pages long, Jonson hardly ever stops for breath, and I'm first on after the interval. It's their last meeting, when Jonson was on his marathon walk to Scotland, and he stopped off at Stratford to tell Shakespeare that the Globe had burned down and also incidentally to touch him for a loan. There's not much love lost between them in the play: Jonson hated the serenity, the success and above all the self-discipline of Shakespeare: he

was more Rabelaisian, in and out of prison four times, but better educated than Shakespeare and determined never to let him forget it – Jonson treated him with a strange mixture of envy and contempt, yet he was the only one at the time who realised that Shakespeare was forever.

Interview by Sheridan Morley, The Times

Once again, predictably, there was a mixed reaction, most of the critics didn't like it much. In long notes in the programme Bond stated he had made his explanations to protect the play from petty criticism. Barry Took fell hook, line and sinker:

. . . I'm afraid Mr Bond, you won't protect your play from petty criticism – not from me you won't.

They do make you laugh, don't they? Critics. They're better than the play sometimes. Later in a long piece Mr Took gets his act together and remembers to review the performances:

Sir John Gielgud plays the bard on a note of sustained melancholy, and frankly I'm not surprised that Judith (Gillian Martell) got so ratty with him. The best scene in the play goes to Arthur Lowe as Ben Jonson, when the two playwrights sit drinking and talking shop, and Jonson tries to take Shakespeare out of himself. The dialogue crackles with inventive phrases and genuinely funny lines, with Arthur Lowe handsomely bewigged and auburn bearded, flourishing his truculent common sense like the banner of an outnumbered but defiant army. All too soon we're back into the plot . . .

Punch

John Barber, writing in the Daily Telegraph liked it, but thought that the great actor had not found a great role, that he was impressive, but under-parted. He too sat up during Arthur's ten pages:

> . . . the theme emerges powerfully when Ben Jonson arrives for a booze-up that ends in his cadging money . . .

Milton Shulman was alright about it, though it wasn't to his taste:

> John Gielgud, with his high dome and neat beard measuring almost exactly our preconceptions of Shakespeare's facial features, bears a concentrated look of contemplative sorrow throughout the entire evening. He is not only a gentle Bard, but a woeful one. Was such a gloomy fellow capable of inventing the glorious clowns and provoking the heavenly laughter that graces so many of his plays?
>
> Indeed this play's major weakness is that it never gives us Shakespeare, but a philosophical argument based on one tiny sliver of the Bard's complex, mysterious and diverse character.
>
> Only occasionally, in a phrase like 'Hell is full of burning scruples,' are we reminded that

this was the world's greatest architect of language. Only occasionally, such as in the drunken exchanges with Ben Jonson, interpreted with dead-pan elegance by Arthur Lowe do we catch a glimpse of the ordinary fellow, stripped of mankind's worries, that Shakespeare probably was most of the time.

Evening Standard

You might think I've been too selective in my choice of newspaper cuttings, but I've searched for ones which slated Arthur, and I can't find any. One letter surfaced which is clearly written from the heart, and so – though from nobody famous – seems to deserve a place here.

Dear Mr Lowe,
Last night I went to see 'Bingo', the play was splendid. Edward Bond <u>must</u> have written the part <u>just</u> for you – and how you make the most of it – <u>if possible</u> you get better and better – I so enjoyed the evening – you made it a memorable one – thank you!

I'm not in London very often these days, but I was glad to catch 'Bingo' – very good luck with it – please do <u>more</u> plays! – incidentally I thought you stole 'The Ruling Class' poor Peter O'Toole didn't stand a chance! – you never told me you could dance!! – a man of many talents!

Take care,

Love Cynthia
(DAD'S ARMY MAKE-UP!)
P.S. Thought you looked divine in that RED wig!

I was nineteen and home from sea, and went along with a comp simply because I knew Dad was really good at playing drunks. I imagine a lot of the play's real meaning went over the top of my simple sailor head but one line came home with me – and forgive me please, Mr Bond, if I misquote you – 'Hate is like a clown with a knife, he must draw blood to get the joke.' It has stayed with me ever since.

Somehow Arthur fitted a whole load of other work into 1973: he played Louis Pasteur in the BBC's splendid production *The Microbe Hunters.* He kept his beard for it – he had a strong beard, snow white. He and Joanie went to Chamonix together for the filming and a very romantic time they had, the altitude suited them both and just for a while I thought I glimpsed young lovers again. Also that year his Mr Micawber in BBC-TV's *David Copperfield* won acclaim from everyone who saw it. He enjoyed Dickens, he read him in his spare moments, and a lot of his own philosophy of life had a Dickensian ring to it.

He did *Dad's Army* for the BBC, *Hopcraft Into Europe* for ATV. A Thirty Minute Theatre, *The Alfred Potter Story,* for Thames. He had met with the children's author and publisher Roger Hargreaves, and had started on the much loved voice-overs to the *Mister Men* cartoons. And lest anyone should be flying too high, commercial clients included Spam, Wincarnis, Victory V, Gold Blend and Walkers Savoury Snack.

*

The tunnel roof has suddenly given way to a cornflower blue Italian sky. There has been a fresh fall of snow in the night, and even where the snow-plough has heaped it at the side of the road it is clean and fluffy. The drive down into Aosta is joyous. There are cars with skis on the roof-rack and brightly coloured occupants heading for the slopes. When I get into the customs compound I lodge my papers and go for a shower. The hot water pummels my stiff neck and shoulders, and I stand under the jet for longer than I'd need to just to get clean. A man in another cubical sings 'Carmen' and I shut my eyes, my head held back, and listen. He sings in Italian, and with the resonance of the shower block, and the passion he feels for his mother tongue and the voluptuous factory girl, he raises the roof. A few drivers gather round, and when he pulls back the filthy curtain, pulling a comb through his black curls we all applaud. The gold caps on his white teeth flash as he smiles and says something in Italian as he pushes through us and out. I catch the eye of a German driver I half know.

He says, 'It ees all in ze day's work!'

Something has happened to me in the night. As I strained to see the red tail-lights of the truck ahead in the driven snow, as the clatter of diesels rebounded off the wet walls of the tunnel, a nerve-jangling cacophony of sound, a metamorphosis came about in me, I have struggled free from my constraining shell. I know now that I love him.

I have resolved to remember my father only up to and including Ben Jonson and to set everything after to one side, not denounced or forgotten, but put in a box that I may not open again.

I go and lie in my bunk, the trucks on the road lulling me to sleep as they go by, vhoom, vhoom, vhoom. I have time on my side now, and I'll drive down by

Genoa and Leghorn, with the warm sea to my right, heading for the Crespi-Snack at Grosseto where one always eats so well for a fiver.

7

'Ham on the bone'
1975–1978

THE year was 1975. They now embarked on the *Dad's Army Stage Show*. David and Jimmy wrote it, Cyril Ornadel did the score. It was a revue of the early war years, and the whole thing lent itself terribly well to the stage. The cast was huge, I hope you'll forgive me if I just list them: Arthur Lowe, John le Mesurier, Clive Dunn, Arnold Ridley and Ian Lavender, of course. Hamish Roughead played Private Fraser and John Bardon Private Walker. Graham Hamilton, Eric Longworth, Norman MacLeod, Bill Pertwee, Frank Williams, Edward Sinclair. Jan Davies played Mrs Pike and Joan Cooper was Mrs Holdane Hart, WVS. Pamela Cundell, Michael Bevis, Bernice Adams, Jeffrey Holland, David Wheldon Williams, Ronnie Grange, Barrie Stevens and Kevin Hubbard. I'm sorry if I've left any out. Eric Longworth understudied Arthur. Debbie Blackett, Peggy Ann Jones, Vivien Pearman, June Shand, Michele Summers, Jan Todd and Alan Woodhouse completed the Home Front. Scene six was titled: 'Radio Personalities of 1940'. Arthur and John le Mesurier did a Flanagan and Allen turn, and

Arthur did Robb Wilton. Joan and Pamela Cundell did the Elsie and Doris Waters' characters, 'Gert and Daisy'. It was a riot and loved by all who saw it.

Anecdotes from this time, and photographs, convince me that a physical and mental change had come about in Arthur. He had put on more weight, he was more often irritable, and an air of general dissatisfaction pervaded.

> Some of the actors involved in the stage show had not worked on the television series and had to accustom themselves to Arthur's uncompromising dedication to the show.
>
> *Bill Pertwee, 'The Life Of Arthur Lowe', Radio 2*

They were playing Richmond when Jeffrey Holland's wife, who was expecting a baby and was up in Coventry, went into labour. There was fear of complications and, checking with the members of the cast who would cover for him, Jeff set off hotfoot for Coventry. As it happened, all went well and he was soon back in Richmond, the proud father of a son. Arthur however, far from being full of congratulations and feeling that Jeff should have consulted with him first, gave him a real rollicking. The show must go on, he said, babies have been born before. Only later did he discover how serious the situation had been for Geoff's wife, and a big bouquet of flowers arrived in her room.

> I mean he was not only Captain Mainwaring in the platoon he was Arthur Lowe the head of the company – he was a sort of overall father figure embracing everything there . . .
>
> *Jeffrey Holland*
> *in 'The Life Of Arthur Lowe', Radio 2*

Joan shared a dressing room with the girls, not of course, with Arthur. He enjoyed this, the loneliness of command; but who had appointed him, no-one was quite sure. I think of him standing on a table, his bowler hat jammed up against the ceiling, ' . . . Right, now leave this to me, I'm taking charge from now on . . . ' Looking at Wilson and saying, 'Times of crisis always bring natural-born leaders to the fore, Wilson.'

The theatrical profession happily absorbs these eccentricities, and a good performance is worth a thousand strange habits. At mealtimes at The Bell Hotel in Thetford or out and about in pubs and restaurants Arthur's culinary quirks had become standing jokes with the *Dad's Army* troupe.

At breakfast he would explain at length to the waitress ('You know, the one with the unfortunate legs') that he preferred his tea weak and his coffee strong. To achieve this more than a few times in a lifetime of touring, at least in British Hotels, is a near impossibility. It was seemingly little things like this, enormities to him, that made him so love Holland and Austria.

'I see you have kippers on the menu. Tell me, are they boil-in-the-bag or are they real swim-about kippers?' This to a gesture with the hand imitating the movement of a fish's tail, as if the intellect of the waitress might not be sufficient to grasp the difference without a little picture to help.

The morning was generally occupied (I'm talking here about days off of course, days when there was time to kill) browsing the antique shops and flea markets for treasures for the 'Amazon' and hunting down the only cigarette either he or Joan would smoke, cork-tipped Craven 'A'.

At lunch,

'I'll have a jambon sandwich please, but tell me, is it packeted muck or is it the genuine Wiltshire?' Jambon in this little scene – played out so many times it became like a friendly bit of life itself – was pronounced 'jam bonne'. Sometimes, with a tough old hand, a train steward perhaps, it was received with a wry smile, more usually with total incomprehension or occasionally with a sneer, if inexperience made the recipient feel disadvantaged.

Afternoon tea, taken in one of the public rooms, brought us back to the weak tea debate. Shortly after a cup of tea, and perhaps a little nap in his chair, accompanied by thunderous snoring and lolling forward, he would set off to change the rooms.

Rarely were rooms right the first time, and even if they were they became not so, as their worst features gradually made themselves apparent.

'Do you suppose,' he would address the receptionist, 'there might be hot water on the first floor?' Or,

'Our room commands the most spectacular view of the service well, do you have one which merely overlooks the sea?' Or,

'I didn't sleep so well. I believe we are next to the rooms of ill repute'.

At six they bathed and at drinks time, which was always seven-thirty, Arthur would phone down and begin a procurement routine which would have made Sergeant Bilko look like a greenhorn. All he wanted were two tumblers containing a double gin each, a slice of cucumber each, some ice in a separate dish, and two bottles of tonic water opened or unopened, but if unopened then with a bottle opener supplied. In all my travels with my father – and so I presume when I was not with him also – he never got the complete works delivered to his room successfully first go.

While he waited for the porter to return with the cucumber instead of lemon, or with the forgotten bottle opener, he would go around the radiators bleeding off the air with a radiator key he always kept in his jacket pocket. He would stand with his hand on the upper part of the radiator, like Dr Cameron attending an elderly patient or like Macphaill nursing the rickety engine of the Vital Spark, and feel the warmth returning, a knowledgeable smile creeping onto his face. It was a complex smile, but its main message was one of compassion for the human failings of the hotel management.

The second gin was always taken in the bar while he perused the menu. In larger hotels where the porter and the barman were not one and the same person the procurement routine would begin all over again. In provincial hotels all this would now have brought them dangerously close to last orders in the restaurant. Joan would need a discreet arm to get her to the table where she would implore the waiter to bring her only the smallest portion because she had the appetite of a bird brought about, she said, by deprivation during the war years. Arthur would look across at her, wincing as he anticipated trouble ahead, wondering how he might coax her into eating something. It was easy to follow his eyes, and so his thoughts, because he wore bifocals. He would tempt her with the whitebait, which she loved to eat but hated to cook, or with the idea of having two starters but no main course. He would have mussels or snails, or antipasto, then a steak or rack of lamb. They would have a glass of white with the starter and then share a bottle of red.

'I'll have the Ruffino', or Macon or on a splash-out night the Beaune.

Joan would command the conversation, often re-iterating a favourite topic such as why so-and-so – one of her protégées – would be just right for the part, didn't he think? Arthur would agree pleasantly with grunts that didn't interfere too much with the due process of mastication. From time to time he would nod off and would be awoken either by a kick under the table or a polite cough from a bemused waiter.

Where they could they would leave the hotel and go into the town to eat. Mostly they enjoyed the company of the proprietor and – where the quality of the meal would be taken for granted – they sought out places that were full and fun and had Italian or Greek characters to enjoy. They would have zabaglione, and Arthur would have an Armagnac and Joan an Amoretti.

Later, up in the room, Joan would be very pissed having drunk well and eaten little. Unconsummated love would slip into self-pity and on into recrimination, and she would crash perhaps on the bed, perhaps on the floor. Arthur would undress her and get her into bed. Then he would get room service to bring up a cold beer, and he would sit on the side of the bed in his vest unable himself to find sleep.

They followed this routine for many years. When it came time to leave they thanked everybody most char-mingly, remembered to tip, forgot their coats, and took the taxi around by the newsagents to buy up any remaining stock of Craven 'A', never knowing what sparsity might lie over the horizon of their lives.

Arthur was now suffering – and so was Joan vicariously – from a then little-known condition called narcolepsy. It is a sleep disorder which affects about one in two thousand, though if the symptoms are mild it often goes undiagnosed. Excessive daytime drowsiness and abnormal REM sleep touch every aspect of the sufferer's life:

> The effect of narcolepsy on its victims is devastating. Studies have shown that even treated narcoleptic patients are markedly psychosocially impaired in the area of work, leisure, interpersonal relations and are more prone to accidents. These effects are even more severe than the well-documented deleterious effects of epilepsy using similar criteria for comparison.
> *Stanford University Sleep Disorders Center*

Sufferers can be helped but not cured by medical treatment. The daytime sleepiness can be treated with amphetamines and the freaky cataplexy, sleep paralysis and hypnagogic hallucinations can be treated with antidepressants. So far as I know Arthur was taking no medication, but the condition had been diagnosed. At first he would nod off if there was no real action to keep his attention, in taxis, at rehearsal when he was waiting to go on. Later it became more sinister, and infinitely more difficult, because he would nod off – cut out would be a better description – in mid sentence or mid action.

It had its funny side.

'The mulligatawny's not as good as it was,' Arthur said, lifting his head out of the soup bowl into which he had crashed.

And it had its sad side too, as he was sometimes mistaken for drunk, which he very rarely was. For work colleagues it meant added complications that they didn't need, but then his performances were still worth it – he was a good engineer. As Jimmy Perry told me:

> But then with electronic editing, I wouldn't say this to anybody else but I'll say it to you, because he's your Dad, with electronic editing, we could cut out the ums and ahs that he did . . . He was very sharp in those days but then as they got older we used to electronically edit something like seventy or eighty little edits, we're talking about seconds, one second or two . . .

Seeking an explanation for Arthur's little dries, it's difficult sometimes to make a clear distinction between his renowned laziness over learning his lines and fleeting attacks of catatonia. When I tell people that he worked with about the narcolepsy, and its symptoms, they often express disbelief or surprise. They make a joke, perhaps because it's a way we all deal with illnesses we don't understand or fear. He made every effort to hide it, though it rapidly became impossible to disguise. It compounded his learning problem because he was quite unable to stay awake for long enough to read a page. Certainly it came and went and wasn't always this bad, but in the last seven years of his life I am not exaggerating when I say that its effects were catastrophic. Jimmy Perry again:

> Don't forget, Stephen, this is very important, your Dad and I had one thing in common:

148

we'd both done years of weekly rep. Now, nobody knows about weekly rep now, it's all forgotten, you know it's all dead and gone. Who cares about weekly rep? But Arthur, I think because he'd had such a pounding, in weekly rep having to learn the part, fresh part every week, was inclined – and I was just as guilty as anyone else – to do an awful lot of paraphrasing. I went in the dressing room, this was when they were doing the show at the Shaftesbury. And your mother said, 'You'll have to learn it Arthur, you know. You can't just wing it.' This was a little thing I'd done for the Royal Command Show.

The *Dad's Army Stage Show* was at the Shaftesbury Theatre when they did Jimmy's 'little thing' for the Royal Variety Performance at the Palladium. There was no space backstage at the Palladium for the enormous star cast that had been assembled, the *Dad's Army* lot found themselves sitting upstairs in a nearby pub, waiting for their call. It really was their finest hour. For John le Mesurier and Arthur the highlight of the evening came when they realised that Count Basie was standing in the wings, enjoying their act. Later, lined up on the stairs, they shook hands with the Queen. She exchanged a few words with Dad, but I don't know what was said.

In February 1976, when they went on tour with the show, Joan went too, and they fell into a routine which they knew and loved. They were welcomed everywhere they went, so much had the nation taken these characters to their hearts. One particular invitation to lunch is worth a read:

Dear Captain Mainwaring,

As the grandson of the Prime Minister who declared war on Germany, I wish to extend to you and your company a very warm welcome to Bath.

I know very well that my grandfather had a profound admiration and respect for the members of the Home Guard, who so gallantly and tirelessly worked for the defence of England.

I write, therefore, to ask if I may have the privilege of thanking you personally on his behalf.

To this end I extend to you and all members of your company (including wives etc.!!) a most warm invitation to visit us whilst in Bath. We have in our house a number of historic documents, possessions, presentations, which I think you would enjoy seeing.

We realise that with so many performances your free time must be very limited and precious, but we should be so delighted to welcome you to our home to pay homage to the soldiers of Walmington-on-Sea, but especially to your own decisive impressive dignified leadership. – to Sgt. Wilson's imperturbable (if somewhat upper-class) loyalty – to Private Jones who forsakes his liver and lights for King and Country – and to dear old Private Godfrey who, despite his physical disability (incidentally we can provide ample facilities) so faithfully soldiers on.

If you are able to accept our invitation (the date and time of your choice) General Elliott

Roosevelt – son of the American President – also wishes to join the party to convey to you his father's profound appreciation and wonder that so few men could so effectively defend our shores – also a Polish cousin of ours, Count Badeni, who served in the RAF wishes to offer you his apologies for that most embarrassing incident you sustained when you were all so cruelly interned by his countrymen.

We invite you to drinks, or lunch or dinner, whichever you can manage. And the only request I make of you is that I may photograph you, bearing in mind your inimitable military style, holding my grandfather's umbrella.

Yours sincerely,
Neville Chamberlain

P.S. I am sixteen years of age and write this letter as the sole male Chamberlain descendant of my grandfather. However, my mother most heartily endorses this invitation and asks me to assure you that you will be received and entertained with the dignity and respect you are due.

Something the *Dad's Army* team shared was a love of cricket. It may be an actors' game, because I can think of a lot who are fond of it. Arthur's own connection can be traced back a long way: the cricket ground at Hayfield really marks the centre of the village. It occupies the river meadow and the cottages hang on the steep sides of the valley overlooking it. The Lowe's cottage was strategically situated just two minutes away from The Railway tavern in one direction and the cricket in the other (four pubs were within five minutes walk of it). A small pavilion, renewed in recent times, a hand roller and the score board, some folding wooden chairs scattered about. The team and the spectators alike wandering around with pints either bought from the makeshift bar in the pavilion or brought over from the The Royal, not a hundred yards away. Northern village life epitomised.

Arthur supported the team and watched the matches whenever he was home. So it was that on Sunday 9 May 1976 touring with the *Dad's Army Stage Show* he persuaded the *Dad's Army* team to play against the village. The show was in Bradford, so it wasn't so very far for them all to drive in a hired bus. The reason for the match was to raise funds for the purchase of the ground by the club – securing the future of cricket in Hayfield. The Gods must have looked kindly upon them because it didn't rain. And the pubs were granted all day opening, a thing dear to Hayfield's heart.

Perhaps what surprised everybody was the turnout. It had been expected that the event would be popular, but no-one had anticipated the three thousand people who packed the cricket ground and the narrow streets, and jostled at the bars awash with beer.

Hodges lost the toss. Well, what can you expect from a man like that? So Hayfield were first in, captained by Ron Heron, their oldest playing member. They scored one-hundred-and-seventy-two.

The evocative cuck of leather on willow is followed in the memory by a ripple of clapping, but this was replaced with good-humoured heckling and cheering as the *Dad's Army* team took their turn at the wicket. It's forgotten now but Arnold Ridley, before he was wounded in the First War, had played football, rugby and cricket for his county and now he had a good innings, third in to bat and scoring twenty runs. He was granted a runner out of respect for his seventy-nine years and the heat of the day, and a girl stood by with a chair so he could sit down from time to time. Bill Pertwee made the best score, forty-nine, and the team was all out for one-hundred-and-forty-seven conceding defeat to Hayfield by a mere twenty-five runs.

Arthur and John didn't bat, they were both under contract for future work and subject to clauses excluding sporting activity, but after they'd inspected the team they worked away in the marquee selling their autographs. At the end of the day the best part of a thousand pounds had been raised. Granny had come down from the cottage, and now Alice took her home. The *Dad's Army* team climbed into their bus and headed back to Bradford, chatting and joking along the way. A lot of beer had been saved from going bad, and they had to stop in a layby to relieve themselves, privacy provided by the bus.

'Oh, we can't have this, no, no,' said Arthur, and instructed the driver to pull ahead leaving a row of men looking furtively over their shoulders.

Joan, first introduced to cricket by her father, had developed a real interest in the game when she worked for Derek Salberg. Most of all she enjoyed the one-day cricket, and she had a small transistor radio and at one time a tiny portable television, so that she could follow it.

The team started work on the radio series of *Dad's Army*. Although it didn't pay so well as television it was great fun for them to do and brought the programme to a whole new audience again. In all, Harold Snoad and Michael Knowles adapted sixty-five episodes for radio.

So much had Joan enjoyed being back in the theatre, and so much had she never wanted that tour to end, she now applied unreasonable pressure on Arthur to take more work that could include parts for her. In a conversation I had with their agent Peter Campbell – who really of all people would know best, having spoken to Arthur almost every day from the 1960's on – I felt Peter wanted to say something, but was unsure of how to phrase it. He didn't know what I had in my head, didn't want to cause offence and shut a door. I egged him on, certain of what he was going to say, hoping he wouldn't dilute the truth:

> You know the last ten years of his career theatre-wise was blown by having to include Joan . . . I could never really talk about it with Arthur . . . was love so blind? He must have known.

They took *Laburnum Grove* together for Triumph Productions and were playing Harrogate before coming into town. Peter got a call from the producer, Duncan Weldon: it can't come to London with Joan in it, he hadn't realised, he said. Peter said Arthur wouldn't come into town without Joan in the show. Peter felt in a terrible position, and it put him under a lot of strain. He couldn't talk with his client about it, he knew exactly what managements meant when they said they weren't satisfied. Peter was – is – a sensitive man, and he felt his own health threatened by a situation that was running out of control.

Laburnum Grove came to London. Arthur enjoyed good crits, Joan's performance was quite simply ignored. A lie was being lived at home now too. Arthur's narcolepsy worsened and Joan's drinking increased. I was actually unaware at the time of the reason for the constant arguments and my father's now obvious unhappiness. I have only discovered all this since. I think – as far as I recall, but I shut my ears to most of it and was away an awful lot – they never spoke of the real problem.

One weekend the thing came to a dreadful crisis point, but nothing was resolved and a workaround was arrived at only by Arthur making a dreadfully disappointing sacrifice.

He rang Peter early on the Monday morning at Barclay House. He sounded dreadful, Peter said he feared the worst, perhaps Arthur was going to sack him, he didn't know. Arthur said he was coming over in a taxi. When he arrived the main lift was out of order. Unable to face the climb up the stairs, he went around the back of the building and came up in the service lift. When he sat down opposite Peter he broke down in tears. He said he'd had the worst weekend of his life.

He had been offered a part by Michael Codron in a play. Michael, who had produced *Stop It Whoever You Are* at the Arts, Arthur had known and respected him for years, and now he was having to turn down Michael's offer because, if there was no part in it for Joan, he couldn't, he wouldn't do it.

In telling a story, especially one as personal as this, there is a danger of losing the perspective of time. Every day of my father's life was not a misery – very far from it – and his motive in making such bitter sacrifices was the love he had for Joanie. Each Valentine's Day and on her birthday every year he gave her the most beautiful lace cards, flowers in abundance and sugared almonds, gold and diamonds in well-chosen settings – things he had gone to great lengths to find, that they should be just right, to express his love as best he could, for his talent lay in expressing other people's words, not uttering his own.

A great volume of other, less personally sensitive, work occupied the majority of the time. There were plenty of personal successes out there still to be had. It was just that the high ridge – in a moment of sad realisation, when one sees the best of the day is gone – had already been attained and now, in worsening weather, there was nothing for it but to make the most of the descent.

One of those great personal successes – something I took notice of from the start – was *Philby, Burgess And MacLean* for television in 1977. He did something most unusual, for Arthur, and started reading up all about Herbert Morrison, the Home Secretary he was to portray. He actually came to look like him in the weeks leading up to the recording of the thing, and though I never saw it, I'm told he was brilliant. Another, the previous year, had been the Ray Galton and Alan Simpson Comedy Playhouse *Car Along The Pass*.

Of all the things that Arthur ever did this is the one that causes people to stop me and say, 'What was that thing Arthur did . . . ?'

It was chosen as his epitaph: they repeated it on the night after he died. I never saw it for many years until I went to see John Newman in 1995. He sat me down in his front room with my son Jack, and we watched it together. John had recorded it from the broadcast so the announcer's voice came, to tell us of Arthur's death, and that this was a tribute. Mona Washbourne, dear old Mona, comrade on so many campaigns with him, played his wife.

It is funny. It's a simple piece, classically simple I mean, and it hasn't dated. I think the reason it still packs such a punch is how incredibly rude Henry Duckworth is to the German.

The characters are in a cable car, which has not yet become stuck half way along the pass. Henry Duckworth, Arthur's character, finds himself sitting next to a dapper German. Duckworth starts making objectionable comments and the German decides to introduce himself . . .

STEINER. Permit me to introduce myself. Heinz Steiner from Baden-Baden.
DUCKWORTH. Really? Henry Duckworth from Twickenham-Twickenham.

It's come full circle. Do most of us not now take Alf Garnett's stance in our heart of hearts?

Jack was a year old when it was made. I watch him, now twenty, as the video plays. His eyes are going around the room, taking in the details, he's interested in John Newman and where he fits into his grandfather's story, but he doesn't find *Car Along The Pass* funny. He's grown up in an age of smart-ass stand-up comedy. Later in John's office he's impressed by so many playbills on the walls, fascinated that this direct, pleasant man is the dynamo behind such a volume of work. We take some photographs and leave and as we walk along through the suburbs, looking for the station, I think what a debt of gratitude I owe the man. It was John who stuck his neck out for them and toured Arthur and Joan here and there, all the way to New Zealand once, so that they could be where they had in some ways only ever wanted to be, together playing the theatre.

The volume of Arthur's work for commercials had now increased to quite an amazing level. Morning after morning he was back down to Wardour Street. It was lucrative work, and he was well respected in the little studios, many of them up twisty stairs in the sleazy quarter. Cadbury, Rawlings, Audi Cars, Qantas, British Airways, Heinz Beans.

They did *Caught Napping* for Triumph in 1978 from the May right through to the September, as well as the film *The Lady Vanishes*. In this remake of the old Hitchcock classic (why do people do this?) Arthur played the Basil Radford part of Charters and Ian Carmichael played the Naunton Wayne part, Caldicott. Elliott Gould and Cybill Shepherd were in the lead roles and it was directed by Anthony Page. Arthur and Ian and Joan had a great time sitting around in Austria while the screenwriter, a harassed George Axelrod, tried to make it work with re-write after re-write. The only parts that didn't get altered were Arthur's and Ian's because George confessed to knowing nothing about cricket.

'Knows nothing about cricket? Oh dear.'

Halliwell's verdict:

> A remake . . . in which everything goes wrong: wrong shape, wrong actors, wrong style (or lack of it). Reasonable adherence to the original script can't save it.

The producer, Michael Carreras, very kindly flew Arthur and Joan to Geneva for a little holiday, and everyone had a jolly good time. Arthur would have dearly loved to have success in films, but he came along at the wrong time.

After *The Lady Vanishes* they were both in the Beryl Bainbridge film, *Sweet William*. Arthur played Captain Walton and Joan played Aunt Bee. Claude Whatham (*Swallows And Amazons* and *That'll Be The Day*) directed, but Halliwell's verdict is just:

> A situation in search of a story makes this slight piece with its wry observations rather less memorable than the average TV play.

It just was not to be. Warren Beatty offered Arthur a part in his film, *Heaven Can Wait*. Arthur would have had to go to America for the filming, something he would have loved, but he turned it down because there was no part for Joanie. There wasn't too much time for regret, because two new TV series came along. Arthur embraced them both, his enthusiasm for a new character as fresh as ever it had been, and his interest in Northern writers as keen as ever. First, *Potter*. Roy Clarke, who had previously written *The Growing Pains Of PC Penrose* and *Rosie*, had now written a thing about a retired sweet manufacturer and dreadful busy body called Redvers Potter. Clarke used his unusual skill, just as we've seen since in *Last Of The Summer Wine*, to construct absorbing episodes around minimal plots. It was a feel-good programme with the feel in the dialogue. John Warner, who played 'Tolly' Tolliver wrote to me:

Each episode of *Potter* would end with a bliss-fully funny scene between John Barron and Arthur, chatting nonchalantly side by side, not listening to each other, and full of non-sequiturs and long pauses, where Arthur's comedy timing showed so superbly. The scene always reminded me of Naunton Wayne and Basil Radford. During the final episodes, when Arthur was beginning to have trouble learning his lines each week, he would rely on 'idiot boards' out of camera vision. But his technique was so subtle, that the viewer would never have known that he had to rely on them whilst he read the lines.

The other new series in that incredibly busy year, a year in which Arthur could literally be said to have been working himself to death, was LWT's *Bless Me Father*. Peter de Rosa had been a priest and wrote these stories around the antics of an anarchic Irish priest to the parish of St Jude's in the fictional London borough of Fairwater. Arthur polished his Irish brogue about the house and slipped into the character of Father Duddleswell for the series. He loved the character, took real pleasure in him, it was back to stuff like W.W. Jacobs for him.

Then, in early summer, Father Duddleswell called in Dr Daley again. The parish priest was now in a position to confirm that there was indeed an outbreak of miracles at St Jude's.

'Donal,' he began, 'what does the Holy Bible tell us about Sarah?'

'Sarah who, Charles?' Dr Daley said, setting his black bag down on the desk.

'Sarah, wife of Abraham.'

'I haven't had a drink all morning, so I have no idea.'

'Jasus,' Duddleswell said, rooting around for the necessary, ''tis as useless as hammering cold iron with a hair of me head.'

Peter de Rosa, 'Bless Me Father'

Arthur never became Redvers Potter, but he did become Father Duddleswell. Peter de Rosa had captured all the pithy speech of a man whose daily life dealt with life itself, and death, and deceit. Arthur was wholly absorbed in the character. The show has dated; the genre – sitcom – has developed out of all recognition since then, so it has never been repeated.

8

'Like a tiny peep into hell'
1979–1982

I HAVE set off in the early hours, so as to have daylight for Genoa and Leghorn. It seems like another life when we were there on the 'Bravo', but it's a life that flickers in my mind's eye and which calls me constantly. My Dad is there, and my Mum, and I'm an innocent, savouring the pleasures of life without complication or guilt. A great future lies ahead of me. If a genie arose from a magic lamp and offered to travel me back to any point in time, I would go only to there.

This great long list of Arthur's engagements, extracted from the little brown book, has got in the way of all that. If I were to investigate the details of every item I would have to live his life for years, not mine. And yet my own life has come out of his.

This brute of a truck thunders on through the dark, and the steering is so light and the seat so comfortable it is as if I am not controlling it at all. Just flying along in a void. As if at the edge of a cliff, I feel compelled to wrench the wheel to the right and career off into the fields. Cigarettes and coffee and a very little brandy and the road. Arthur and Joan gave me so much, they gave me life, and now I wish I could dig them up and give them back theirs.

*

They nearly bought – or bought-into, I don't know – the theatre on Brighton Pier. Dating back to 1897, it was quite big and with work needing done. I pleaded – silently – with my father to go for it, but he knew nothing of business and feared it. Joanie could have found a niche there, could have done what she did well, which was stage-management, set design, art direction. Arthur could have had a new project, appeared there sometimes, commuted to London. The sea air could have blown through their lives. I don't know enough about it to tell you – or to explain to myself – exactly why they didn't do it.

They just didn't have much luck with piers, as Harold Snoad explained:

'*It Sticks Out Half A Mile* was a radio series – written by myself and Michael Knowles after the end of the radio versions of *Dad's Army*. I took the first episode to your Dad – on the boat at Teddington – and he loved it and said why didn't I try to get it off the ground for television. However, I couldn't get the powers-that-be interested so we decided to settle for it being a radio series. We made a pilot episode with your Dad and John le Mesurier, and the radio hierarchy said they would like us to write a series. We were in the process of doing so when we heard the sad news that your father had died.

We assumed that was the end of that idea. However, as I was leaving St Martin-in-the-Fields after your father's memorial service, your mother stopped me, took me aside and told me that your Dad was really enthusiastic about the series and that he would have wanted us to go about it in some other way. We re-wrote it to star John le Mesurier, Ian Lavender and Bill Pertwee. We recorded ten episodes – which were well received – and were about to be asked to write some more when John le Mesurier died! Ironic isn't it?'

*

I have timed it just right, and as the new sun clears the hills the light strikes down onto the Gulf of Genoa and sparkles like so many sequins on a blue frock. It may be the brandy or it may be the blinding light, but I drive along over those raised sections with tears streaming down my face.

On the movie we shot there are horse-drawn carts in the streets of Genoa and there are brightly coloured trams, there's a shot of Arthur in white chinos and a striped sports shirt and Joan in a new silk scarf. She had a dream about a place called Poggibonsi and we all had to go there on a train.

*

Fed up with hotels and missing their beloved 'Amazon', in 1979 it was put to me that we should sail to various ports around the coast where they coincided with dates that John Newman would fix. *Beyond A Joke,* a new comedy by playwright Derek Benfield, was chosen.

We had used 'Amazon' like this three years before in 1976 when I was married to Susan – Jack's mother – and Jack was just a baby. It wasn't without its tensions: even a baby as accommodating and as cheerful as Jack needs his own routine, the daily cleaning demanded by the 'Amazon' to keep her shipshape was punishing. There was shopping and cooking to do, and then for Joan and Arthur an interminable taxi ride from Shoreham to Eastbourne to play the theatre. (Later, when Brighton Marina was built, Eastbourne became a more practicable date). Brown old ladies, leathered by the wind, made great company when they came down, bright blue eyes like buttons on an old bridgecoat. Arthur was able to do what he did best, offer spontaneous hospitality, drop the business of the day for the comfort of a deckchair and pass around glasses of fizz. In everything he did he acted out the role; if he brought someone a drink on the deck then he would have a white cloth draped over his arm, once again the steward on the SS 'Adriana'.

The plan worked out, and the first booking was for the season at the Shanklin Theatre on the Isle of Wight. He and Joan were to play together, and Benfield's *Beyond A Joke* held promise. I had 'Amazon' down in Falmouth working on the *Onedin Line* for BBC Television, and we arrived at Cowes on the 2 July, the night Arthur and Joan opened. They joined two days later when the vessel had taken up her moorings in Folly Reach.

We had a small 'rooberized dinghy', an inflateable of the type favoured by yachtsmen and powered by a

Seagull outboard motor. Late on each afternoon we would venture forth in this thing for the Folly Inn pier. Arthur in his yachting cap and reefer jacket, Joan in her reefer jacket wearing a silk scarf with anchors on and clutching her harmonica, myself and maybe Bear, who was my companion in the 'Amazon' for ten happy years. With such a crew we had pitifully little freeboard and Arthur would usually arrive at the Folly with a wet bottom, but with his gusto for disparaging other people's boats undampened. He could never grasp the way in which the voice carries over water, especially when raised above the clatter of the outboard.

'Look at that poxy little thing,' he would say in a voice that could fill the Palladium.

'I don't know how people could put to sea in a tub like that.' Or, worse,

'I wonder if that clown knows what he looks like.'

We had hired a car and we would now set off across the island, taking the backroads because Arthur prided himself on his knowledge of 'little ways through'. (He knew a way through Paddington Station parcels office that cut off a bad junction and he would always direct his cars that way, he got to know the porters and they would wave cheerily as his Mercedes or Granada swept through. When the narcolepsy hit him, the driver would still go through that way, but with the comatose Arthur slumped forward in the front seat, the scene looked like something from a mystery thriller.) This summer I was their chauffeur – Arthur wasn't allowed to drive anymore because of his nodding off – and I was required to drive very slowly because Joanie, perched on the edge of the back seat, was a nervous passenger. She would play a phrase on her harmonica, and we would be challenged to name the tune. If we missed three in a row we were in trouble and Arthur would escape by going to sleep, leaving me to defend our corner. Joan would now sink back into her seat and practise a particular phrase over and over until she was certain she had it right.

The island was very gentle and green in July, and as we made the steep descent into Shanklin, here was the English seaside. A broad bay with the waters of the channel lapping a shingle beach, a pier, boarding houses and the theatre. From his vantage point in the passenger seat Arthur could survey the whole scene from Timothy Whites to The Novelty Rock Emporium.

'Oooh, it's like a tiny peep into hell,' he'd say as he glimpsed three fat women in their flowered summer frocks screeching with laughter at the dirty postcards, covering their mouths with podgy hands. Tonight's audience.

The first of two high season theatrical attractions that herald an Island breakthrough into big-time summer entertainment opens on Monday at Shanklin Theatre. Many big seaside resorts will certainly be envying John Newman's plum booking of Arthur Lowe to star In Derek Benfield's latest comedy *Beyond A Joke*.

Arthur, truly a household name via his celebrated TV appearances in *Dad's Army*, *Potter* and *Bless Me Father*, is currently also enjoying a new wave of success on a much bigger screen. *The Lady Vanishes* is doing very nicely thank you, and it features Arthur and Ian Carmichael re-creating the Charters roles made famous by Basil Radford and Naunton Wayne.

The strong supporting cast for *Beyond A Joke* contains many well-known TV faces. These include Honor Shepherd, Joan Cooper (the real life Mrs Lowe), Peter Greene, Annette Woollett, Brian Tully, Jane Elliot and Vyvian Hall. This production looks certain to bring out unprecedented summer crowds to the Shanklin Theatre. Good luck to Arthur Lowe or should I say Captain Mainwaring or is it Father Duddleswell or even Redvers Potter.

John Hannam, Isle of Wight Weekly Post,
29 June 1979

They were surrounded by friends. Christopher Bond, who they knew from their early days in rep and who had been a co-writer on *The Last Of The Baskets,* directed. Vyvian became their constant companion and it was he who was to perform the last great and thankless task for Arthur. Everybody settled in for the duration.

My valuable cargo discharged at the stage door, I would then have the evening to kill. Bear and I might lie on the deck if it was warm or sit in the Folly Inn, a very welcoming island-happy place. We made lasting friends there on the island.

At night, after the show, I would help them from the car and down to the dinghy, bobbing at the jetty. If there was a moon the light it cast would sparkle on the water and Joanie would say, 'These are my diamonds, these are my rocks, you can keep all your theatre lights'.

Back on board there would be gins and a cold supper with wine, brandies, tantrums, cold beers and standing on the deck in the cool early hours with cigarettes, and in the morning it would all begin again.

One Sunday, with no performance, Arthur and Joan invited Honor Shepherd for the day. Honor was Bob Dorning's wife, and and it was good to have her in the show, when you thought of how Arthur and Bob had played together in *Pardon The Expression,* and how narrowly Bob had missed the boat in the casting of *Dad's Army.* We slipped our moorings early and steamed down to the west. All told we had few of these days.

Joanie took up her sea-spot on the bench in the deckhouse, her things arranged about her, silver bosun's call on a chain around her neck, packet of Craven 'A' and gleaming brass Zippo lighter, harmonica, newspaper folded open at the crossword. Arthur stood on the bridge or took a trick at the wheel, arctic convoy coat kapok-cosy in the hot summer sun. Honor elegant beside him, vibrant and romantic, all her favourite men short and fat with whiskers.

Derek Benfield wrote these words to me:

> Having always admired Arthur Lowe's perform-
> ances, especially that of Captain Mainwaring in
> *Dad's Army,* I was a very delighted playwright
> when he agreed to appear in my comedy
> *Beyond A Joke* for Newpalm Productions in 1979.
> Arthur had the amazing ability of being able to
> give every part he played his own special
> brand of magic. But he was a great respecter of
> an author's lines and never changed one word
> of the text, never indulged in the awful game of
> ad lib and 'cod corpse', but managed to make it
> seem as if he had freshly minted each phrase
> every evening. And always he remained in char-
> acter. I never tired of watching his performance.

Arthur was the master of the pause. I can remember sitting in front with John Newman one night in Eastbourne, and at one particular moment a pause which had always been lengthy seemed to go on for ever, and we thought 'My God, he's going to miss it!' But, of course, he didn't. The laugh that came was even bigger than usual! Such timing only comes with comic genius, and Arthur was certainly that.

In the September, on the 23rd, we sailed for Jersey. John Newman had booked a late season run there with the same play. It was late in the year to be crossing the Channel in a hundred year-old yacht that had risen from the ashes. Alan Cundell, the genial Folly harbour master, was with us and there aren't many entries in the log, so I may have thought it was stuff I didn't want our underwriters to read, ever. We slept that night in the blessed lee of Cherbourg's ugly breakwaters, and it was the 27th before Arthur's old bus rolled her way in past Elizabeth Castle and we put our lines ashore in the commercial basin at St Helier.

There were Arthur, Joan and Honor at the landing steps, relieved to see us. They had been staying at the Caledonian Hotel, but now they were pleased to forsake the comfort of the hotel for their hard berths aboard the 'Amazon'. Our reception on Jersey was not a warm one. Lord and Lady Docker had had their yacht here shortly before us, and they had made clear their resentment at having to keep shifting berth in order to accommodate the comings and goings of the coasters. We on the other hand enjoyed the coasters and shifted 'Amazon' promptly at every request. By the end of our stay we had restored some goodwill with the harbour master and his men. There is a great rise and fall of the tide in the Channel Isles, so the horrid little rubber duck had to be employed again to ferry Arthur, Joan and Honor to and from the steps. I'm not sure why we weren't all drowned.

I had cooked all summer for my parents and their friends and it was a joy to arrive in Jersey and shop in her markets, the horn of plenty spewing forth a great variety of fish and vegetables. Arthur loved to come with me, and we spent happy mornings together choosing prawns and scallops, crabs and shark steaks, yellow capsicums (long before they were ever seen on Tesco's shelves) and tomatoes as big as your fist (before anyone dreamt up 'beefsteak tomato'). The summer in England had been warm, but here it was hot every day, the sort of hot that dispels all guilt at drinking a cold beer at ten in the morning. Arthur loved to dress crabs, and he would spend an hour or two standing in the galley patiently picking the meat out of every last crevice. These he would proudly present to members of the cast he had invited for lunch. Joan preferred tinned sardines, or baked beans, and would sometimes taunt him,

'If everything is cloth of gold, up goes the price of shoddy.' It cut him to the quick, because he loved good food and had worked hard for it.

I too used to tease him, but in an underhand way, which I am not proud to remember. He loved lamb, and new season's English lamb was an annual ritual to which he subscribed with great joy. I would sometimes substitute a piece of frozen New Zealand lamb, and while I could never have openly lied to him he never even thought to ask. Instead, flourishing the carving knife and the steel like the fat chef of a Trust House Forte carvery, he would hack in skilfully with cries of,

'Ah, English lamb, nothing like it'.

The good times, like the bad times, can't go on forever. They played the theatre in St Helier through the October and the weather held. One day they went to the airport and flew for home and other work. Bear and myself found ourselves silently alone again aboard the empty 'Amazon'. It was a relief and like Masefield's crowd we 'were free to quit the ship'. We sat in the sun, much lower in the sky at midday now, drinking beers in our own time. It was too hard to try and organise a crew so we sailed for England alone, borne up on a high swell that announced the coming of winter.

Gin, gourmandising and the open sea did not really mix, Arthur found. 'Amazon' would have had to be the 'Queen Mary' to meet his needs in these departments. His friend Bob Patterson at the boatyard had said from the beginning,

'Holding on with one hand, and a corned-beef sandwich in the other? That's not for you, Mr Loo.'

So it was that I was asked to take the 'Amazon' up to Paris: April in Paris, they said. The unfolding splendour of the River Seine, moored in the centre of Arthur's second favourite city, Joan's third . . . It did sound good. 'Amazon' was lying at Tough Bros yard at Teddington Locks, and we moved her to the drying berth for inspection before the long voyage. There was too much slack in the stern bearing so it was removed for remetalling. A bend was suspected in the short intermediate shaft so this was taken ashore to be checked. We left Teddington on the 26 March and dodged gale after gale on our voyage to le Havre. The days advanced.

Arthur and Joan crossed on the overnight ferry from Portsmouth on 9 April. Holiday time was precious time to them, and the gales had somewhat disrupted their plans.

They hadn't slept at all well on the ferry, and to make matters worse they had been standing on the jetty for forty minutes hailing the boat while I snored peacefully on, unaware of the difference in the hour. When, tousle-headed, I came alongside with the dinghy, I thought I recognised the look on my father's face. I think he nearly said,

'Stupid Boy!'

We waited for low water and then set off up the Seine towards Honfleur, the sun came out, a light breeze chased along behind us and all was well. The Rouen pilot cutter ran alongside us, her captain out on the bridge wing studying us through binoculars. She was a handsome old vessel of about three hundred tons, I stared back through my binoculars as sailors do. He put his hand up to his ear.

'Friendly chap,' Arthur said, saluting in a nonchalant way he had got from Noël Coward in *In Which We Serve*.

'I think he wants to speak to us on the radio,' I said.

'Oh', said Arthur, disappointed. Then,

'Ah', as he realised that here he was witnessing the first action scene in the drama of our voyage.

'Bonjour, Monsieur,' said a friendly voice, 'Go to Channel 10, please.'

We went to Channel 10.

'Bonjour encore, you are a very big vessel for just twenty-one tons register. If you are bound for Paris you will need to take a pilot, I think.'

My eyes met my father's. His days in rep had taught him not to get flustered, his boxing as a young man had taught him to think, right how are we going to handle this one?

The last thing we wanted was a pilot: he would be expensive, he would curtail our freedom and as Arthur said later,

'He would probably have stunk of garlic.'

'Tell him we're only going up to Honfleur, we can play it from there,' he said squinting his eyes.

'Captain,' I said into the handset, 'we are bound for Honfleur. We can see the pierheads from here.'

There was an uncomfortable pause. We both wondered if he had seen the morning paper: it carried an article about us.

'O.K. Messieurs "Amazonnes", bonnes vacances,' and he put up his helm and steamed away to the west.

Honfleur was heaven on earth for Arthur and Joan. Bear's brother Rupert joined us, so now we were a complement of five. Holiday-makers strolled around the tiny harbour. With French deference they did not stare like their English counterparts at Poole or Torquay. The 'Chef du Port' occupied an extravagant medieval tower which dominated the sea wall and gave him such importance he could afford to be friendly towards foreigners. Every colourful doorway was a café, and around the quay artists in berets took three-quarter-finished canvases from their hessian bags and ingeniously avoided the difficult task of painting the newly arrived boat into their pictures. We stayed for three days so charming was it, until late one evening, in a tactical operation masterminded by Arthur, we slipped out under cover of darkness past the pilot cutter, at anchor a mile or so to the north.

And then, carried up on the powerful flood tide, the black waters boiling beneath us as the incoming salt shouldered its way into the downcoming fresh, our troubles began. The intermediate shaft bearing, disturbed at Teddington, began to run very hot and needed constant dousing with a bucket to prevent the grease from catching fire. Not to alarm Joan, I whispered this news in Arthur's ear. We examined the chart together in the red glow of the deckhouse nightlight, like the scene from *A Night To Remember* where Kenneth More as Lightoller peers at the compass minutes before the 'Titanic' hits the berg. Pilings, where motor barges would moor while they waited for the locks, were marked right beneath the Tancarville Bridge.

'How urgent is it that we stop?' Arthur asked, calm and weighing the odds.

'We can't go on to Rouen without fixing it', I replied. 'There's nowhere to anchor up the river, and deep-sea ships use the channel'.

Bravely facing the fact that his first holiday in years was going seriously wrong, Arthur agreed. The problem he had to face, much trickier than mine, was telling Joan.

Ten minutes later, as I went alongside the pilings, in the dark and the swirl of the tide I misjudged the approach, and the bowsprit became hopelessly entangled in some ironwork. 'Amazon' hung for a moment, balancing the forces that acted upon her. Something had to give. Helpless I stood beside my father on the deck, and we watched as, with a heart-breaking crack, the bowsprit parted about halfway along its length.

Freed now, we could again manoeuvre. Not wasting a second Arthur moved quickly about the deck to help get the boat secured alongside. We worked silently recovering the wreckage and getting it stowed on deck. He and Joan, with sagging, defeated shoulders, made their way to their cabin. I settled in the deckhouse with a blanket and waited for daylight.

Engineers came, big cheery fellows in the ubiquitous blue fatigues of the French artisan. Three of them peered down into the bilge at the offending bearing, their broad backsides pointing skywards. Never very far away, everybody's humour began to return, fuelled by the sun, coffee and pain au chocolat. Fascinated by the men and the work in hand, Arthur began to enjoy himself again.

Three days later we proceeded upriver, the cliffs of the lower reaches throwing back the intense light of Northern France. Past Rolleboise where the Americans first advanced. Up through Rouen, big foreign-going ships, Russians, Indians lying to the quays heavily listed, cranes busy, on now with our masts and funnel lowered for the city's deceptively low spans. Queuing for locks, moving at the pace of the river and not a jot faster, held in a Gallic time warp.

We fell into a pleasant routine of steaming in the mornings, lunching and then maybe knocking off a few more kilometres in the late afternoon before finding a resting place for the night.

Late one afternoon we were approaching a mooring place at Le Vieux Moulin in Vernon. It seemed to get no nearer, and after a few minutes we realised we had come to a graceful stop on a mudbank. We turned astern for a while but 'Amazon' was stuck. Help not being immediately to hand, normal conversation resumed. Arthur bowled a googly.

'Of course, when Major-General Ivor Thomas was here he didn't get stuck.'

'Who?'

'Major-General Thomas. He was in charge of the operation to cross the Seine, liberate Vernon and create a bridgehead for the advancing allies.'

We all gathered round, doubtless with our mouths a little bit open, like Pike.

'Oh, yes. He didn't get stuck.'

'Yes, but he wasn't in an eight-foot-draft steam yacht,' replied Joan.

'True,' said Arthur pursing his lips.

Arthur paced the deck, Joan retired to her cabin.

'The Wiltshires, fine body of men. And the Somerset Light Infantry, that was Arnold Ridley's regiment y'know.'

At that moment a péniche we recognised, a very rusty, dirty one, skippered by an unshaven garrulous fellow in shorts and a vest hailed round the bend. He had passed us a day or two before and had been on the quay at Honfleur, so we knew him quite well. He preferred to steer with his feet, leaning right back on his stool looking at pornographic magazines. We had dubbed him El Pirate. There was a sticker in his window which said, 'Les bateliers sont sympathiques'.

'I will tow you off ze mud', he shouted, 'price one bottle of veesky.'

Again Arthur's eyes met mine in silent consultation. He gave a little nod, almost imperceptible, to indicate his approval. The big barge nudged up to us, and we connected a thick hawser to the stern.

'Doucement, monsieur,' I entreated him, wondering about the sign in the wheelhouse window.

As he took the weight, not so much with the promised simpatico, but with something more akin to brute force, Joan appeared on deck. There was a twang as the hawser came tight, a bang, and she was just in time to see the whole taffrail, still supporting her beloved ensign staff, fly through the air and land splosh in the river. She took immediately to her bunk with a bottle of gin, while Arthur – if his patience was wearing thin he didn't show it – worked for the second time that trip to recover the wreckage and square away the deck.

'I will try again!' shouted El Pirate. He could see his bottle of whisky fast slipping away.

'No you bloody well won't!' Arthur shouted back, reddening around the collar.

A Dutchman and his apple-faced wife, cheerful and competent, kindly drove their spotless barge past us at full tilt and the wave they put up allowed us to come off under our own power. Later that evening, when Bear's brother had repaired the damage and the ensign staff was restored to its proper place, we sat round and ate dinner.

'Damned Froggies,' said Arthur, and everyone's feathers seemed back in place.

The various delays had now made us hopelessly late for April in Paris. The river in early spring was very lovely, and the days warm, but sadly the pressure was on, not helped by having to run the engines slower to avoid increasing vibration from 'Amazon's ailing shaft. Days that should have been passed in rapture, as the lush banks and the pretty houses with their landings slipped by, were punctuated with staccato conversations about time, money and failure.

They accused me. I accused them. When our big guns were spent we peppered each other at short range with irrelevant little grievances. One sad Sunday, in a beautiful place where the cliffs rise sheer from the river and buzzards wheel on the hot air of the afternoon, I mutinied and would not take the 'Amazon' on.

'Look, just get the fucking boat back to England,' my mother said and, with nothing but a holdall and a credit card, Arthur and Joan set off to find their own way home.

They must have been terribly, bitterly disappointed.

By mistake – I never did inherit my father's timing – I met them in the town three hours later. They were filling in time until their train came. We exchanged a few words, politely, like strangers. I left them, arm in arm, discussing something in a jeweller's window.

Unfortunately for me the next conversation I had with him was to arrange a banker's draft to pay for the repairs. We had limped back to Le Havre where we could dry out and find the real cause of the problem: the bearing we had had remetalled. It had simply fallen to bits, and the shaft was turning with three inches of slack in the old lignum vitae from 'Amazon's' steam days.

The engineers in the blue overalls were back, laughing and joking, unabashed as they had done what we asked them to a month before and done it well. The English actor and his family were clearly mad, vive la différence. Gauloise in the middle of pursed lips, eyes screwed up against the smoke, Fernand measured with a micrometer. He drew on the hull with a piece of chalk to explain his plan of action and did some calculations accompanied by a low whistle to indicate that it was going to be very expensive. Once the repairs were done I telephoned Dad again.

In an upbeat voice he made arrangements to meet us in Paris in a week's time and so it was that we all had May in Paris together. 'Amazon' was moored to the Quai de Conti, right opposite L'Île de la Cité.

Arthur was in happy and generous mood and took us all to dinner at an expensive restaurant where we had to queue for an hour. He loved every minute of that wait, jostled by waiters who were excruciatingly rude to the queue, insolently polite to the diners. He struck a friendship with a New Yorker who shared his love of good food. They agreed it was going to be worth the purgatory as they scrutinised each steaming plate as it headed, flamboyantly held aloft, to its proper table. As we got nearer to getting seated we were rewarded with Martinis, and when we sat to eat it was every bit worth it. I thought at that moment that my father had gained a new sophistication from somewhere. Perhaps our relative positions had shifted after the dust-up, and he was allowing me to see him in a different light.

Joan was buoyed up too, carried along on Arthur's enthusiasm, but I felt she was damaged, we were damaged, our relationship never really to recover from the days that led up to the mutiny.

Arthur and Joan flew home, and Bear and Rupert and myself brought 'Amazon' back by the Dunkirk Liaison.

It was well into July when we ran up on the tide through London's bridges and back to our familiar berth at Teddington. A lighterman whistled across the water.

'Orl right? 'Ow's Arfur?'

9

'Get off home'

1981–1989

DAD'S *Army* seemed all wrapped up. The great runs of repeats hadn't begun then. We hadn't entered the dark age of TV Comedy, so the programme didn't yet shine forth like a lighthouse on a winter's night. It was fondly remembered, and the actors who survived were tarred with its brush, but it was yet to become a legend.

John le Mesurier, now not at all well, wrote Arthur this kind letter:

> How very nice to hear from you, I feel very lonely without you all sometimes, and am sad not to be busy, as you are. But the slightest physical exertion puffs me out, and I've long accepted that my defection was inevitable.
>
> Mind you, if we were all called on location to Thetford tomorrow, I'd be there!

As the letter implies, Arthur was taking on as much work as ever.

He played in *Hobson's Choice* at the Lyric Hammersmith, and no sooner was this finished but he had me move 'Amazon' to Brighton, so that he and Joan could live on board while they played Eastbourne for Newpalm with their now tried and trusted *Beyond A Joke*. He did an extraordinary volume of commercial work, sometimes going in a taxi from Brighton to London in the morning and returning in the mid afternoon for a nap before setting off for the theatre. He had many major advertising clients now, amongst them Guinness, Volvo, Shell, Barclays Bank, the GPO and British Rail. He still kept his old client Cadbury. He remained a master of the voice-over. He often got it done on the first take. Where subsequent takes were done, invariably the client bought the first one. Similar work, but in a different genre, continued with more voice-over for the *Mister Men*.

There was a new television series for Thames, *A.J. Wentworth BA,* in which he was to play a prep-school master who is weak on discipline and prone to disaster.

If there is indeed such a thing as Punch humour, then Mr Charles Pooter stands as its personification, a mild, bumbling, totally honourable, totally ineffectual pompous ass who engages our sympathies because he means so well and yet performs so ill. We are currently being offered the great treat of seeing one of Pooter's most distinguished descendants transmitted into television. A.J. Wentworth, BA, was the creation of one-time deputy editor of this magazine, H.F. Ellis, who conceived one more in the long line of fictitious English schoolmasters.

Wentworth is a Mr Chips on roller-skates, and in the light of that fact it is revealing that James Hilton said of Wentworth that, 'He will surely be propelled into the small, exalted list of great fools by a friendly kick in the pants from his readers.' Wentworth is a Mr Quelch without the minatory gift, a Mr Smugg without the energy, and his experiences at Burgrove School have never quite been forgotten by those who first came across them in Punch. Two years ago he made an unpredictable but triumphal comeback in hardback, and his career has now blossomed further, thanks to another representative Punch writer, Basil Boothroyd, who has adapted the stories for ITV.

What makes a quietly pleasing episode into something altogether more auspicious is the fact that the man born to play Wentworth was actually chosen to play him. If there is such a thing as Punch humour, then the late Arthur Lowe was its histrionic embodiment, a wonderful personification of all the elements of that style of humour, the mumbled asides, the deadpan face, the solemnity battling against an indifferent and occasionally malevolent world. In the opening episode last Monday, Wentworth was victimised not only by his pupils but also by his colleagues, who hide books from him and generally conspire to undermine the last few shreds of his authority by feigning innocence even as they laugh at him. The essence of Wentworth's martyrdom is that he expects nothing better and never complains, and in this art there has never been anyone in the television age to come anywhere near Lowe, who sadly died during the making of the series.

Benny Green, Punch, July 1982

I found a letter from H.F. Ellis to Arthur:

Dear Mr Lowe,

I thought you might like, in moments of leisure (if any), to refresh your memory of the character of A.J.Wentworth as revealed by his private thoughts and ruminations in the book – most of which, since soliloquies unfortunately went out with Shakespeare, can hardly be reproduced in the TV adaptation.

When the plan to make a TV series was first mooted I immediately felt that the combination of pomposity, earnestness, tetchiness, self-righteousness and basic good nature, which you so brilliantly portraited as Captain Mainwaring in *Dad's Army*, would be just right for Wentworth. I was, as you can imagine, delighted when I heard that you had agreed to play the part, in addition to reading the book on the wireless.

My own feeling is that there are more visual opportunities in the second part of the book, and I hope that the series will follow the old fool into retirement. But it is early days yet.

With all good wishes,

Yours sincerely,
Huntley Ellis

Wentworth was a really charming series, yet another of those little mysteries, it hasn't been seen since.

Lindsay Anderson was casting again, this time for *Britannia Hospital*. Lindsay sent him a postcard from Derbyshire:

> Forgive my delay in thanking you for your greatly esteemed and invaluable and cherished appearance in *Britannia Hospital* . . . The rushes were excellent . . . we completed 'Principal Photography' on Monday, and I have taken off for a few days in the country before plunging into editing. Hope the studio goes well – and I am looking forward to the Victoria Palace at Christmas time -

The thing at the Victoria Palace that Lindsay was looking forward to was the panto, *Mother Goose*. Joan had a part too and though the theatre was less than twenty minutes in a taxi from home, they checked into the Goring Hotel – a rather comfortable, family-run place just behind Buckingham Palace – so that they didn't have to sort out meals or anything. I think it's a sign that they were low on steam, because they loathed hotels and liked to be home.

John Inman has some memories of that time as he related to Bill Pertwee in his radio tribute to Arthur:

> At rehearsals he couldn't get into the habit of calling me madam, or miss or missus. And when Mother Goose comes out of the magic pool and she's all beautiful and no-one recognises her we had a scene where Arthur had to

say, 'Allow me to introduce myself dear Madam'. And at rehearsals, every single day because I was in trousers and a jacket he would say, 'Allow me to introduce myself dear Sir'. And we used to go, 'No Arthur, no. It's Madam because I shall have a frock on.' He got there eventually. And about the second night or the third night he did it. There I was, high heels, eyelashes, big red mouth, big red wig and he said, 'Allow me to introduce myself dear Sir'. And pulled the place apart. And after it had all died down I said, 'Well that's two and a half hours gone for a Burton'. The wonderful thing is that every year since I have got whoever is playing the squire to do exactly the same line, so that we get the same laugh.

When I look at Arthur's list of engagements for 1982 it's one of the quietest starts to any year yet. There's not much listed at all. I remember he said he felt very tired after doing the panto and that he didn't think he'd do one another year.

When he took R.C. Sherriff's *Home At Seven* for Newpalm, and when it went to the Alexandra Theatre at Birmingham owned by Derek Salberg, he didn't know that he was just about coming full circle. There was a part in it for Joan, so they were happy and in a theatre owned by the man they'd worked for in their very early and happiest days together.

In the morning of what was to be Arthur's last day alive, he went with company manager Roger Richardson to do a forces broadcast at BBC Birmingham, then they went on to Pebble Mill:

. . . It was Arthur's favourite city anyway and, as you know, he loved playing Birmingham and he'd done one or two interviews before the show even though it was a matinée day. And we didn't start until about 10 – 10.30 in the morning. BBC Radio first, and then BRMB. The BBC were dropping some tapes on the Task Force which was steaming down to the South Atlantic. Tommy Vance, I think, was the DJ on the day. It was a live link-up between Birmingham and London and they were recording it for the British Forces thing. The DJ was sort of asking questions and Arthur was just sort of ad-libbing and doing the Captain Mainwaring. You know, to sort of gee up the troops, which he desperately wanted to do, and he really enjoyed doing it actually. Then it was off to Pebble Mill, and I'd organised a bed for him at Pebble Mill, so that he could have a sleep and a sandwich, before he was on the air at half-past one.

At Pebble Mill Arthur gave everybody a fright:

He gave us all the heebie-jeebies a little bit because I'd asked Pebble Mill to put a bed in so that he could have a sleep, you know, just to lie down because it was lunch time, then one of the Floor Managers came after me. 'We've lost Mr Lowe!' And he'd gone off on a walkabout. They were in a real flap because you know . . . live TV . . . Arthur had disappeared out of his dressing room. I was outside in the street looking for him. He was having a wander around the park. I said 'Arthur, you're on in about five minutes!' And of course the Floor Manager was going absolutely crazy.

In the afternoon Derek Salberg rang to see if Arthur wanted to go to the cricket the next day. He said he was too tired, that he'd stay and rest, but that Joan would go. Later they did the matinée. No-one suspected anything was wrong, in fact Arthur seemed on rather good form, I ask Roger if it was true he had egg and chips for his last meal:

> Yes. It was in the queue in Birmingham, because the two guys who run the little café, and I mean . . . down backstage there, there's like a crew room sort of stroke green room at the stage door of the Alexon, it was all the Falklands carry on at the time of course, and I remember I was sat watching the TV with your Mum and er . . . and your father always in the queue as well, which was also really quite strange, looking back on it, but back down the corridor there was a lot of people queuing up, but he was cracking jokes and things and he was going through all his range of characters. He was doing a Mr Swindley in the line, he was doing a Captain Mainwaring and he was, you know, just cracking jokes with whoever was waiting in the line; quite extraordinary really considering what happened, you know . . . a bit later.

Arthur collapsed reading a book in his dressing room. Joanie was in the dressing room next door and was called through.

'He's done this before,' she said.

An ambulance came and took him to Birmingham General Hospital. He never recovered consciousness.

Joan was given the choice of cancelling the performance, but she insisted that they carried on. Arthur would have wanted it, she said. Vyvian Hall was understudying him and went on with the book. It was especially hard for Vyvian. As a close friend he was mortified by Arthur's collapse, and as an actor he had the impossible task of trying to replace him in the show.

In the morning Arthur was pronounced dead, from a stroke.

After Joan, Roger Richardson was the next person to know:

> . . . The phone rang at about twenty to six in the morning and of course I thought, 'Well to hell with you.' So before anyone else could get in, I rang the BBC newsdesk, 'This is official that he's . . . that Arthur Lowe's died. You can check with the hospital if you want.' And I explained who I was and I said, 'Well look, I've got to ring IRN now.' Which I did and told them, so that they would get it hot on the wire. And I had a quick shower and by the time the ten past six came on, there was a news flash on the BBC radio.

And that was the news flash that my mate Shaun heard the morning I awoke on the boat, moored in Folly

Reach. Joan and John Newman talked and quickly decided to continue with the run. It wasn't just about Arthur, it was about everybody in the cast, people who relied on the production for their livelihood. Roger had a strange experience that evening, a bit of black comedy really, that – looking back – seems poignant:

> And then that evening when the show was on, a BBC producer came down and . . . and I'll tell you this thing because I mean . . . you know . . . and he said to me, this BBC producer who was drunk basically, and I mean he threw a pu . . . he started pun . . . having a punch up with me in the dress circle bar with Mike, with Michael Bullock. Yes, because I . . . he accused me of, of, of . . . that it was my fault that Arthur had died. I had killed him because I had asked him to do too many interviews.
>
> *Roger Richardson, Company Manager*

Whatever did bring about Arthur's early demise, it certainly wasn't doing too many interviews. His old pal from the Duke of Lancasters, Bill Bateman, made the funeral arrangements. Joan, knowing she would be with the show in Ireland by the day of the funeral, went out to the crematorium and wrote in the book, 'Loved by millions.'

Myself and Bear, Bill and Phyl Bateman, Peter Campbell, John Newman, Derek Salberg – there were just a handful of us at the funeral. We went to a pub or a hotel after, I can't remember. There were obituaries in all the papers, but the most memorable thing was put very simply by Clive Dunn, 'We'll miss him terribly.'

*

I've tipped my drums of chemical, in a yard not unlike the one where I loaded them. Some other English drivers are queuing to tip but I don't go over to talk to them, this moment is mine. I go to the payphone and call the office: I'll be loading for home in Turin next week, the girl says. I head north now, to a place I know that overlooks the bay. It's a small hotel, and I'll eat calamari fritti and drink the rough white wine with a plug of olive oil in the neck and sleep a dreamless sleep in a real bed.

The ghosts are laid now. If they walk at all, which I doubt, then they walk in happy places like Hereford and Thetford, in the alleyways and doorways of the Royal Court, along Wardour Street. I can make this my last trip. I don't need the money any more and anyway the trade is changing. I won't come this way again.

Guido, the landlord's little lad, is grinning at me, his head on one side. He doesn't want anything, he's just sharing this moment with me, celebrating life itself. I walk over to the low building with its red roof and climbing vine, and my father's words are ringing in my ears.

'Get it done, hope it'll be good – and get off home!'

Epilogue

ARTHUR will live on forever but, ironically, it won't be his best work that is seen. His best work will live on for a while in the hearts and minds of those people who saw him at the Arts, at the National and at the Royal Court. Students of cinema may from time to time watch *This Sporting Life* or *The White Bus.*

Joanie lived for another five years after Arthur died, but her life was nothing without him. In many ways their love had been the Destroying Angel, it destroyed her now. She didn't renew the lease on the flat in London but moved instead to the cottage at Hayfield. In doing so she cut herself off entirely from her friends, a few of whom visited her when they could. One young actor, Robbie, was a regular companion for her but even with him she argued. If David or myself went to see her we couldn't stay long or else the conversation would move away from the acceptable and towards confrontation. Without Arthur she was, simply, desperately unhappy.

She went out through the electric curtains to the music the same way he had done. The body meant nothing to either of them: neither died believers. The ceremonies – what they were, sick, shallow – were laid on for us, not for them. Yet we didn't want them either.

195

It took some years before I could go and clear her dressing table on the boat. There wasn't much there: a few hair grips, a gadget for getting fluff off your frock, a faded polaroid of them on the boat when they were playing Shanklin, and a jar of edible pebbles. I put them in a bin bag with her clothes and chucked them out. They weren't really a soldier's things.

Our memories are not static like those of most families, they are dynamic because we see Arthur, and sometimes Joan, on many Saturday tea-times on the box. We read about Mainwaring in the papers all the time, cited as everything that is sound about old-fashioned Britain. People – strangers – come up to us in the street and talk about him in quite personal terms. We are so used to it that it bothers us not at all. In fact, it's really rather nice.

Appendix One

A RTHUR *wrote this résumé of his career to go in the* Bingo *programme. It's particularly interesting because he selects the things he feels were waypoints in his career up to that time.*

ARTHUR LOWE entered the professional theatre after serving in the Middle East during the war, where he became deeply involved with Forces Entertainment.

His first professional engagement was with Frank H. Fortescue at Manchester, where he met his wife, actress Joan Cooper. After this, he worked with the Hereford Repertory Theatre Company and with many of the near London reps, including Bromley, Richmond and Croydon. His earlier experience also included a great deal of touring in plays such as *The School For Scandal*, *The Linden Tree* and *Miss Mable*.

His West End debut was in *Larger Than Life* at the Duke of York's Theatre. His many West End appearances include the musicals *Call Me Madam*, *Pal Joey*, and *The Pajama Game* during which period he managed to accumulate a great number of broadcasting credits.

Perhaps he really came to notice in *A Dead Secret* with Paul Scofield at the Piccadilly Theatre, which attracted great critical acclaim, as did his performance in 1961 in

197

Henry Livings's play *Stop It Whoever You Are* at the Arts Theatre. The Royal Court has played its part in Arthur Lowe's career, and his début at this theatre was in another Henry Livings play *Kelly's Eye*. Amongst his notable performances at this theatre were the John Osborne play *Inadmissible Evidence* in 1963 and *Soldier's Fortune,* in which he scored a great personal success in the role of Sir Davy Dunce.

Television audiences know Mr Lowe's work well from his many successful television series – the most notable of which is the highly successful *Dad's Army* for the BBC. This series has transferred to the large screen and to radio with equal success.

Other television work includes guest appearances in the *The Morecambe And Wise Show, The Val Doonican Show, Call My Bluff, Doctor At Large* and *Hopcraft Into Europe*. He starred in a series of Ben Travers farces for the BBC, a comedy thriller series entitled *It's Murder But Is It Art?*, also for the BBC, a BBC Drama documentary entitled *The Microbe Hunters,* in which he portrays Louis Pasteur, and *Churchill's People,* BBC TV.

Films include *This Sporting Life, The White Bus, If . . . ,* and *O Lucky Man,* all directed by Lindsay Anderson, *The Bed Sitting Room* and *The Rise and Rise of Michael Rimmer*. He co-starred with Peter O'Toole in *The Ruling Class,* for which he received great personal acclaim, and *Man About The House*.

He has just completed an engagement with Sir John Gielgud in *The Tempest* at the National Theatre, playing Stephano.

Appendix Two

THE list of engagements that follows is taken directly from the small brown notebook which Arthur kept from the day he started for Frank H. Fortescue. In some places his handwriting was hard to read, so I have interpreted as best I can. Obviously, over a period of forty years, he was sometimes more careful than others. There may, therefore, be mistakes, or entries which don't seem to make sense now. Sometimes he made an entry when he started rehearsals, rather than when the show opened or was transmitted. Where there were multiple instances of a series or commercial for a particular client, I have only listed it only once.

1945

Theatre
Bedtime Story

1946

Theatre
Flare Path
Uncle Harry
Whispering Gallery
The Wrong Number
The Fake
It Happened At
    Blackpool
The Letter
Smiling Through
My Wife's Family
Sunshine Sisters
There's Always
    Tomorrow
Uncle Sam's Relations

I Killed The Count
The Case Of Lady
    Chamber
The O'Mara Mystery
Almost A Honeymoon
Jane Eyre
Sport Of Kings
The Last Of Mrs
    Cheyney
Quiet Weekend
The Old Man
Candida
Trilby
Artificial Silk
This Sex Business
Lady Be Careful
Flame Guard
Arms And The Man
While The Sun Shines
Ignorance
Pink String
Portrait In Black
Scandalmongers

Radio
Children's Hour:
    Know Your County

1947

Theatre
How Are They At
    Home
Blithe Spirit
Pink String
While The Sun Shines
Ghosts
Worm's Eye View
Wishing Well
Flare Path
The Corn Is Green
Caste
Quiet Weekend
This Land Of Ours
Jane Steps Out
Ten Little Niggers

The Importance Of
  Being Earnest
This Happy Breed
See How They Run
Candida
Acacia Avenue
Poison Pen
Kendall Wakes
Jupiter Laughs
Bank
Letters To A Lady
Your Brother George
The Door Opens
The Years Between
Wuthering Heights
The Hasty Heart
Bird In Hand
Arsenic And Old Lace
Fools Rush In
The Sacred Flame
By Candlelight
The Wind Of Heaven
This Blessed Plot
Grand National Night
Too Young To Marry
Night Must Fall
Claudia
Some For Love
The Ghost Train

1948

Theatre
Dear Brutus
The School For Scandal
The Linden Tree

Radio
Adventure Unlimited
Mrs Dale's Diary

Films
London Belongs To Me
Flood Tide

Miscellaneous
The Personal Touch

1949

Theatre
Fly Away Peter
The Linden Tree
The Merchant Of
  Venice
Life With Father
You Never Can Tell
Too Young To Marry
Queen Bongo
The Perfect Woman
The Years Between
The Magic Cupboard

Radio
Return To The Black
  Country
Father Brown
The Digger Experiment
Evacuation From
  Dunkirk
The Fool's Saga
The Prayer Book
The Trial Of Lord
  Byron
Miss Mable

Films
Kind Hearts And
  Coronets
Stop Press Girl
Poets' Pub
The Spider And The
  Fly
Until Tomorrow
The Intruder
The Wealth Of The
  World

Miscellaneous
Until Tomorrow

1950

Theatre
Off The Record
Little Women
The Hasty Heart
The Happiest Days
  Of Your Life
Mountain Air
Edward My Son
Clutterbuck
Jane Steps Out
Wind Of Heaven
The Middle Watch
Musical Chairs
Larger Than Life
The Romantic Young
  Lady
Dear Brutus
What Anne Brought
  Home
Bonaventure
QE Slept Here
You Never Can Tell
The Constant Wife
She Stoops To
  Conquer
The Third Visitor
Too Young To Marry
Castle In The Air
When We Are Married
Murder At The
  Vicarage
Man And Superman
The Party For
  Christmas
Just William

Films
The Cage Of Gold

1951

Theatre
The Silver Box

Peg O'My Heart
One Wild Oat
Hassan
Champagne For
    Delilah
A Streetcar Named
    Desire
Count Your Blessings
The Holly And The Ivy
The Wishing Well
Lace On Her Petticoat
Design For Living
The Bishop
    Misbehaves
Who Is Sylvia?
The Case Of The
    Frightened Lady
Totty
On Monday Next
The Apple Cart
Charley's Aunt
The Barretts Of
    Wimpole Street
Party Manners
The Importance Of
    Wearing Clothes

Radio
The Young And
    Ancient Man

Television
I Made News: Big
    Band
To Live In Peace
I Made News: These
    Hands

Films

Miscellaneous
Daimler Hire
The Yorkshire Way:
    We've Got It Taped
The Way To Holiday

1952

Theatre
Black Coffee
Call Me Madam

Radio
G-Men No.4
F.E.B.: Plain English
F.E.B.: Citizenship
The Mounties
BBC Schools: For The
    Fourteens

Television
Blundell's Club
One Way Genie

Films
Dan Dare
The Good Companions

Miscellaneous
The Yorkshire Way

1953

Theatre
See How They Run
Murder At The Ministry
To Cristobel
Life Begins At Fifty
The Marriot Mystery
Glad Tidings

Radio
PC 49
Men Apart
The Orange In The
    Tree
Cavemen Of Whitty
Murder In Three Acts
Mr Muddlecombe, JP
Deep Sea Towage
Wilfred Owen

Television
An American
    Gentleman
Sounding Brass

Films
The Mirror And
    Markheim

Miscellaneous
BMK Carpets (two
    commercials)

1954

Theatre
Wake Up! (revue)
Meet Mr Callaghan
Pal Joey

Radio
Brontë Country
Henry Hall's Guest
    Night
Capetown Riot
BBC Schools: History 2
BBC Schools: Jennings
    At School
Children's Hour
BBC Schools: History 1

Television
The Old Grad
My Uncle Rolls
TV TeleClub: Friend
    Sally
The Three Musketeers
The Olive Jar

Films
Death Keeps A Date
Dangerous Money

Miscellaneous
Road Safety
Austin Motors
Commercial:
　Sharps Toffee
I Am A Car
Commercial:
　Summer County
Commercial: Cadburys

1955

Theatre
Witness For The
　Prosecution
The Pajama Game

Radio
BBC Schools:
　Current Affairs
BBC Schools: Talks
Looking For Trouble
Mrs Easter's Parasol
Five To Ten
Auntie Rides Again
Sovereign Lords
BBC Schools:
　Current Affairs
Q Theatre: The New
　Romans
Travel Talks
BBC Schools:
　World History 2
Daily Telegraph
　Centenary
BBC Schools:
　Looking At Things

Television
Children Of The New
　Forest
Passage Of Arms
Valley Of Shadows
The Wise Cat
The Prince And The
　Pauper

Films
The Reluctant Bride
Three Women For Joe
One Way Out
Breakaway
Who Done It?
John Dark

Miscellaneous
Audible Slide Films
Daily Sketch
Regentone (two
　commercials)
Sharps Toffee (two
　commercials)

1956

Theatre

Radio
BBC Schools:
　Geography
BBC Schools: Current
　Affairs
BBC Schools: Science
　In the Community
Return To The Black
　Country
BBC Schools: Country
　Schools
Five To Ten
BBC Schools: Science
　In The Community
BBC Schools: The
　Jacksons

Television
Sixpenny Corner
Gordon Honour

Films
The High Terrace
The Green Man

Table In The Corner
The Black Tide
Stranger In Town

Miscellaneous
Shopping With the
　Stars
Milk Board
Black & Decker
　(two commercials)
Dampson Cream
Bisto
Bread
The Handyman

1957

Theatre
A Dead Secret

Radio
BBC Schools: People
　Places And Things
BBC Schools: History 1
Five To Ten
Intrigue
This I Believe
You're Confidential
Children's Hour

Television
Six Red Hens
Report To Downing
　Street
Sounding Brass

Films

Miscellaneous
Quaker Oats
Sunfresh Tonic Water
Horlicks

1958

Theatre

Radio
Five To Ten
BBC Schools
Q Theatre:
    Test Of Truth

Television
Murder Bag
Come Rain Come
    Shine
Disturbance
You Were There
Freedom For The
    Prisoner
Murder Bag
Time Out For Peggy
Leave It To Todhunter
All Aboard

Films
Dial 999
The Boy On The
    Bridge

Miscellaneous
Wrigleys
    (two commercials)
Horlicks
Yorkshire

1959

Theatre
Ring Of Truth

Radio
The Silent Brothers

Television
The Diamond Bird

Films
Follow That Horse
The Day They Robbed
    The Bank Of
    England

Miscellaneous
Norman Baker
John Haddon

1960

Theatre

Radio
Tumbledown Dick
BBC Schools:
    Geography
Spycatcher
BBC Schools:
    Senior English
Five To Ten

Television
Lord Arthur Savile's
    Crime
Boyd QC
Once A Crook
A Night Out
The Long Way Home
Beyond The Horizon
Ladies Of The Corridor
After The Party
For The Love Of Mike
Robert Tavenor,
    Deceased
No Hiding Place
Sheep's Clothing
The Stranger
Coronation Street

Miscellaneous
Cadburys

1961

Theatre
Stop It Whoever You
    Are

Radio
Children's Hour
Five To Ten

Television
Coronation Street
Three Live Wires

Films
Go To Blazes

Miscellaneous
Wrigleys

1962

Theatre

Radio
Inspector Scott
    Investigates
Schools
Five To Ten
Schools: Current Affairs
Schools: Science In
    The Community
Schools: Adventures In
    Music
The Weavers

Television
Z Cars
Leading The Blind
Maigret
So Many Children
Zero One Series:
    Murder On Cloud 7
The Third Man
Coronation Street

Films
This Sporting Life

1963

Theatre
Kelly's Eye
The Tulip Tree
The Farmer's Wife
Inadmissible Evidence
A Cuckoo In The
   Nest

Radio
Where The Difference
   Begins
Five To Ten
Schools:
   The Bible And Life
The Day Dumb-
   founded Got His
   Pylon
Nothing On The Clock
The Desperadoes
We'll Think Of
   Something Yet
Schools: Science
Schools: People And
   Places

Television
The Snag
Mr Pickwick
Coronation Street
The Case Of Carrott
Armchair Theatre
Coronation Street

Films

Miscellaneous
Wrigleys

1964

Theatre

Radio

Television
Coronation Street
Pardon The Expression
   (dry run)

Films

1965

Theatre
Foursome Reel

Radio
I Want To Be An
   Engine-Driver

Television
Coronation Street
Pardon The Expression

Films
You're Joking Of
   Course
The White Bus

1966

Theatre
Foursome Reel
The Soldier's Fortune

Radio
Bosom Of The Family

Television
Pardon The Expression
Turn Out The Lights

Films

Miscellaneous
Bird's Custard
Wrigleys

1967

Theatre
Lock Up Your
   Daughters
Baked Beans And
   Caviar
Marya
The Dragon

Radio

Television
Bad Business
The Avengers
Armchair Theatre
Schools: The Golden
   Age

Films

Miscellaneous
Boots

1968

Theatre
Home And Beauty

Radio
Wednesday Play:
   A Meeting In
   Middle Age
Schools:
   The Bible
Schools:
   Books, Poems, Plays

Television
Dad's Army
Schools: Why Danny
  Misses School
When Robin Was A
  Boy

Films
If . . .
The Bed Sitting Room

Miscellaneous
Fairy Stories

1969

Theatre
Ann Veronica

Radio
Late Night Extra
The Government
  Inspector
Open House
Today: Saturday
  People

Television
A Voyage Round My
  Father
Rogue's Gallery
Simon Dee Show
Some Will, Some Won't
Give Me Your Word
Dad's Army
World In Ferment
This Is Your Life
Noël Coward's Birthday
  Programme
The Cilla Black Show
Tommy Cooper Show
A Cup Of Kindness
Val Doonican Show
Turkey Time
A Cuckoo In The Nest

Films
A Whole Lot Of Trouble
Spring And Port Wine
Fragment Of Fear
The Rise And Rise Of
  Michael Rimmer
It All Goes To Show

Miscellaneous
Huntley & Palmers
Songs Of The Second
  World War
Vim
William Web Ellis Are
  You Mad?
Cambridge Cigarettes
Lyons
  (two commercials)

1970-71

Theatre

Radio
Second Time Around
Desert Island Discs
Woman's Hour
Parsley Sidings
Charlie Chester
Childrens' Interview

Television
Dickens Spectacular
Plunder
Dirty Work
Dad's Army
Rookery Nook
She Follows Me About
Holiday Startime
Doctor At Large
The Morecambe
  And Wise Show
The Last Of The Baskets
Dad's Army Christmas
  Special
Quiz Ball

Films
Dad's Army
The Ruling Class

Miscellaneous
Barclays Bank
Lyons Pie Mix
Shell Oil
The Furniture Show
Florida Orange Juice
Spam
  (three commercials)
Bournvita
Green For Go
Walls Ice Cream
Butter Council
Brooke Bond Tea

1972

Theatre

Radio
Late Night Extra
Sounds Familiar
Parsley Sidings
Junior Choice
Open House

Television
It's Murder But Is It Art?
Dad's Army
Harry Secombe Show

Films
O Lucky Man
Theatre Of Blood
Adolf Hitler, My Part In
  His Downfall

Miscellaneous
Butter Council
Black & White Whisky
My Little Girl
Gold Blend
  (two commercials)

1973

Theatre

Radio
Shindig

Television
The Moira Anderson
  Show
Thirty Minute Theatre:
  The Alfred Potter
  Story
Blue Peter
Omnibus
No Sex Please We're
  British
Bunclarke With An E
  (not transmitted)
Dad's Army
St David's Homes
  Appeal
Call My Bluff
Hopcraft Into Europe
The Microbe Hunters:
  Louis Pasteur

Films
You'd Better Go In
  Disguise

Miscellaneous
Trophy
Electricity Board
Raleigh Toys
Spam
Wincarnis
Victory V
Walkers Savoury Snack
Gold Blend

1974

Theatre
The Tempest
Bingo

Radio
Open House
Interview
Schools:
    Inventing A Poem
Home Guard
Interview
The Impressionists
Late Night Extra
Kaleidoscope

Television
Blue Peter
The Generation Game
Dad's Army
Under The Garden
David Copperfield
Call My Bluff

Films
Man About The House
Mister Men

Miscellaneous
Tetleys Teabags
Barclays Bank
Viscount Biscuits
Clearasil
  (two commercials)
Cedarwood Aftershave
Williams & Glyns Bank
Ultra TV
ABL Biscuits
McVities Biscuits

1975

Theatre
Dad's Army Stage Show
Royal Variety Show

Radio
Open House
Dad's Army
Interview

Start The Week
Forces Network
A Christmas Carol

Television
The School For
  Scandal
Foster Parents
Black And White
  Minstrel Show
Dad's Army
Nationwide
Jackanory

Films
Royal Flash
The Bawdy Adventures
  Of Tom Jones
Mister Men

Miscellaneous
Benson & Hedges
Marie Elizabeth Sardines
Birds Custard
Townsend Thorenson
Cadburys
Rawlings
Colmans Mustard
  (three commercials)
Flooring, Bubble &
  Squeak (two
  commercials)
Coffee Compliment
  (two commercials)
Cecilia Lemon
  Squeezer

1976

Theatre
Dad's Army Stage
  Show, Tour
Laburnum Grove

Radio
Penny Soup
It Gives Me Great
    Pleasure
Open House
Diary Of A Nobody

Television
Bill Brand, Prime
    Minister
This Is Your Life:
    Arnold Ridley
Marty Caine Show
Terra Firma
Pebble Mill, Interview
Look North, Interview
South Today
It's Child's Play
A Likely Story
Car Along The Pass
Cottage To Let
Aquarius
On The Move
Look North
Calendar
Dad's Army Xmas
    Special
Jackanory
Be My Guest

Films

Miscellaneous
BBC Filler
Tower Diamond Pans
Instep Foot Deodorant
Roger Hargreaves
    Timbuktu
Jaffa Cakes
North West Gas
Unipart
Blood Donor
British Airways
Pan Am
Baco Greenhouses
C.O. of I. Safety Film
Rank Training Film

1977

Theatre
Laburnum Grove

Radio
Start The Week
Open House
Interview
Interview
Jack de Manio Presents

Television
The End Of Civilisation
Your Move
Philby
Daphne Laureola
Going For A Song
John le Carré
    Promotion
Dad's Army
Pebble Mill: Story
Our Show
Emu's Adventure For
    Christmas
Jackanory
Morecambe And Wise
    Christmas Show

Films

Miscellaneous
C.O. of I. Training Film
Colmans Mustard
Tizer
Paper Bags
Daddy's Sauce
Cadburys
Rawlings
Cavendish Book
    Promotion
Audi Cars
Roger Hargreaves
    Timbuktu
Euro Advertising
    Company

Sense Of Humour
Stilton Cheese
Children's Stories
Qantas
Wash-Ups
Cadburys Hanky-Panky
Chartered Bank

1978

Theatre
Caught Napping

Radio

Television
Much Ado
Potter
Bless Me Father

Films
The Lady Vanishes
Sweet William

Miscellaneous
Toblerone
Heinz Beans
Marine Safety
    Equipment
Cadburys Cream Eggs
Rawlings
British Rail
National Mutual Life
Craft Magazine
John Reece Children's
    Stories
Toys
BTB Training Film
Laskys

1979

Theatre
Beyond A Joke

Radio
Woman's Hour
Open House
It's Patently Obvious

Television
Potter
Bless Me Father
The Plank
The Little Yellow
    Idol
Len And Jerry Show

Films

Miscellaneous
Bank of Hong Kong
Potter Promotion

1980

Theatre
Beyond A Joke

Radio
The Dock Brief
Woman's Hour
The Soldier's Fortune
Birmingham Symphony
    Xmas Concert

Television
Potter
Sebastian
Bless Me Father

Films

Miscellaneous
Harveys Bristol Cream
Butter
British Airways
Electrolux
Mister Men
Youngs
Parker Pens

1981

Theatre
Hobson's Choice
Beyond A Joke

Radio
Interview
Childrens' Progs:
    Bumble Bees

Television
A.J. Wentworth B.A.

Films
Mister Men
Britannia Hospital

Miscellaneous
Granny Bonds
Concorde
    Lawnmowers
Walkers Crisps
Swinton Insurance

Volvo Motors
    (three commercials)
Cadburys
GPO
BR
Dunlop Outdoor
    Games
Guinness
Bristol & West Building
    Society
Car Magazine
Prima Vera
LifeGuard
Shell
Martin Stores
Barclays Bank

1982

Theatre
Mother Goose

Radio

Television
Nationwide
Looks Familiar

Films
Mister Men: The Little
    Misses
Wagner

Miscellaneous
Talver
King Frog

Index

INDEX